WE HEAR THE
CHRISTMAS
Angels

WE HEAR THE CHRISTMAS Angels

TRUE STORIES OF THEIR PRESENCE

Edited by Evelyn Bence

GuidepostsBooks™
New York, New York

We Hear the Christmas Angels

ISBN 0-8249-4704-5

Published by GuidepostsBooks, 16 East 34ᵗʰ Street, New York, New York 10016
www.guidepostsbooks.com

Distributed by Ideals Publications, a Guideposts company
535 Metroplex Drive, Suite 250, Nashville, Tennessee 37211

GuidepostsBooks and *Ideals* are registered trademarks of Guideposts, Carmel, New York.

Library of Congress Cataloging-in-Publication Data

We hear the christmas angels : true stories of their presence / Evelyn Bence, editor.
    p. cm.
Originally published: Carmel, N.Y. : Guideposts, c2004.
ISBN 0-8249-4704-5
1. Christian life—Anecdotes. 2. Angels—Anecdotes. I. Bence, Evelyn.
BV4517.W4 2006
242—dc22

2006005590

Jacket photograph: Angel Musician (fresco), Forli, Melozzo da (1438-94)/Vatican Museums and Galleries, Vatican City, Italy, Giraudon/www.bridgeman.co.uk

Designed by Marisa Jackson

Printed and bound in Italy

10   9   8   7   6   5   4   3   2   1

ACKNOWLEDGMENTS

Every attempt has been made to credit the sources of copyrighted material used in this book. If any such acknowledgment has been inadvertently omitted or miscredited, receipt of such information would be appreciated.

All Scripture quotations, unless otherwise noted, are taken from *The King James Version of the Bible.*

Scripture quotations marked (NIV) are taken from *The Holy Bible, New International Version.* Copyright © 1973, 1978, 1984 International Bible Society. Used by permission of Zondervan Bible Publishers.

(Continued on page 258)

CONTENTS

INTRODUCTION

O little town of Bethlehem,
How still we see thee lie!
Above thy deep and dreamless sleep
The silent stars go by. . . .

W e hear the Christmas angels." I couldn't think of a better overall description of the true stories gathered for this collection: stories of men, women and children who heard—or saw or sensed—a special message from God that came at the Christmas season or has direct application to this joyous, hopeful time of year.

You may well recognize the title of this volume as a line from the last verse of the Christmas carol "O Little Town of Bethlehem," which poetically summarizes the biblical birth of Jesus and its effect on us, even today. Both Gospel accounts of the Nativity, Matthew and Luke, mention the story's angelic moments. The archangel Gabriel appears to Mary at the Annunciation. Joseph receives angelic instructions in dreams, as do the wise men. The shepherds hear a heavenly birth announcement followed by a whole host of angels singing, "Glory to God in the highest."

From the stories collected in this book, you'll see that God's angels—

messengers—are still delivering tidings of comfort, presence, protection, and joy, particularly at Christmastime.

* The generous customer who allows waitress Coryne Wong-Collinsworth to fly home for Christmas.
* The jar of jam that mysteriously appears in Eileen Fick's fruit cellar.
* The stranger who gives Eric Lenihan his belt to make a tourniquet that saves the life of a soldier on holiday leave.
* The Christmas morning when Janice Brooks-Headrick, alone on a work outpost, awakes to the music of "Joy to the World"—but the radio isn't even plugged in.

These are just a few of the Christmas miracles you'll read about in these pages.

Now, two thousand years after Jesus' birth, does God dispatch more angels to earth in December and January than in other months? The answer is impossible to calculate, but it does seem that during the holiday season people are particularly attuned to spiritual messages and insights. We are sensitive to need—our own and others'. We look for grace. We try to spread goodwill. We hope for joy. Even when the "busyness" of the season threatens to overwhelm us, we are aware of a special heart-tug, often prompted by hearing the seasonal music—the carols—we learned as children. "Silent Night," "O Come All Ye Faithful," "Hark the Herald Angels Sing" and, yes, "O Little Town of Bethlehem."

Having settled on the book title, I pulled out a hymnal and studied the five verses of "O Little Town of Bethlehem," looking for words, phrases or ideas that might help me organize the gathered stories. What a delightful surprise! Within the poem itself I found aspects of angelic roles and messages—shining light, whispering hope, watching with love, conveying peace, blessing with gifts, opening the door to faith—that frame the book's outline.

Most of the stories in this volume are contemporary, in that they've taken place within our lifetime. But first let me bring you one story that sets the stage for all the rest, the story behind the carol, "O Little Town of Bethlehem." The words were written in 1868 by a famed Episcopal priest, Phillips Brooks. And the music? Where did it come from? The title of the story, "The Angel's Song," gives a hint and gives new meaning to the line in the carol's first verse: "Above thy deep and dreamless sleep . . ."

Whether you pick up this book in December or July, read on. As you turn every page, rejoice in the ultimate message of Christmas. The Lord has come. His name is Emmanuel—God With Us. He came as a baby, born in a little town named Bethlehem. And through the presence of the Spirit of God, he abides with us every hour of every day.

—EVELYN BENCE

THE ANGEL'S SONG

RICHARD W. O'DONNELL

A week and a half before Christmas in 1868, Lewis Redner, choirmaster of the Church of the Holy Trinity in Philadelphia, sat at his desk studying the music his children's choir would sing for the holiday service. *Oh, how the children need practice!* thought the choirmaster as he considered the pieces they would be performing. He heard footsteps coming down the hall and looked up to see the church rector, Phillips Brooks. From the expression on his face, something was up, Redner could tell. *I hope nothing has gone wrong,* he thought. *I don't have time for problems.* "What can I do for you, Phillips?" he asked.

Brooks handed Redner a sheet of verse. "Do you think you could set this poem I've written to music?" the rector asked. "I would like the children to sing it at the Christmas service."

Three years prior, Brooks had traveled the winding, dusty road to Bethlehem on Christmas Eve. He'd often talked about the trip and had delivered some of his most memorable sermons about it. Looking down at the little town from atop the hills of Palestine, Brooks was overwhelmed by the miracle that had taken place there so long ago. Now he had finally written a poem about it. A lovely poem, as far as Redner was concerned. But how would he make the time to do it justice? Phillips Brooks was an important man, admired all over America. Not only was he a talented writer whose sermons were printed and sold in bookstores, but he was also a magnificent speaker. With Brooks at the pulpit, the church was always filled. And Redner? Redner was just a simple organist. Who was he to say no to the great Phillips Brooks?

"I will try to compose the music," Redner promised.

When the rector was gone, Redner sighed, wondering when he would have a chance to sit quietly and work on the project.

On Sunday, five days before Christmas, the choir would have its final rehearsal for the special service. Anything that was to be sung would have to be ready by then so the children could have a chance to prepare. "Have you ground out that music yet?" Brooks asked Redner late Friday afternoon.

Redner shook his head. "I will do what I can tomorrow," he promised. "I have set some time aside."

Brooks was disappointed, but he tried not to show it. "If you are unable to compose the music," he said gently, "I will understand."

On Saturday Redner sat down at his desk, but his mind was filled with the mighty anthems his choir was to perform, and he could not concentrate on the rector's simple poem. He was interrupted by other business: A choir robe was missing, there seemed to be a problem with the organ, he ran out of ink for his pen.

After working late into Saturday night on the choir's music, without much more thought on the rector's poem, Redner crawled into bed exhausted and frustrated. Phillips Brooks would not get to hear his poem on Christmas Day. *I can't write this music,* Redner thought as he fell asleep.

If You want it sung at the Christmas service, Lord, You will have to write it Yourself.

Deep into the night, Redner awoke. Did he hear singing? Redner opened his eyes. Someone was whispering a tune in his ear. Redner listened, transfixed, until the singing stopped. Then he lit a candle and looked around the room. He was alone. Seizing a piece of paper from the nightstand, he quickly jotted down the song he'd heard. *One day I will find the perfect words for it.* With a smile on his face, Redner snuffed the wick and closed his eyes.

The first thing Redner saw the next morning was the piece of paper beside his bed. Looking it over, he realized that the simple tune was just right for Brooks's equally modest poem. Redner thought of the piece as "The Angel's Strain," giving credit where credit was due. He could already imagine the children singing it.

At the Christmas service in 1868, the congregation of Philadelphia's Holy Trinity Church heard the debut of Brooks's Christmas poem:

O little town of Bethlehem,
How still we see thee lie!

Brooks was overjoyed when he heard how Redner had come to write the music. Lewis Redner never became a famous man like Phillips Brooks, but Brooks made sure he would always be remembered by giving the music its own name. In fact, it can be seen in hymnals today. "St. Louis" the tune is named, for Lewis the choirmaster, who heard the angel's song.

CHAPTER ONE

SHINING LIGHT

Yet in thy dark streets shineth
The everlasting Light . . . .

One of my favorite paintings of the Annunciation is by Henry Ossawa Tanner. The Virgin Mary, sitting on her bed, looks much like any self-conscious, suddenly startled teenager. And the Archangel Gabriel? He is portrayed as a vertical panel of yellow light—miraculously announcing the coming of the "everlasting Light."

The angel-messengers in these stories are not heard but seen, transforming a dark night or situation—guiding in a December storm, comforting a dying boy and his family, and saving a farmer's life. The last story is written in simple language, as if for a child. Its main character, ten-year-old Kari, asks her mother, "Do angels . . . bring good news to ordinary people like us?"

Her mother's response? "They did on the first Christmas. . . . Why not now?"

Exactly. Why not now?

—E. B.

LEAD, KINDLY LIGHT

ANNA PENNER
AS TOLD TO HELEN GRACE LESCHEID

Anna Penner, a German Mennonite, grew up in Ukraine,
which was occupied by Russians in 1922. Then during World War II,
her village was invaded by Germans, then taken back by Russians.
To escape the crossfire, Anna, her sister Neta, and other German refugees
left Ukraine. That's where we pick up her story,
at age forty, haunted by the fear of war and displacement.

In March 1944, our train rolled into the station in Ratkersburg, a small Alpine town in German-occupied Yugoslavia.

To accommodate us, the Germans displaced the local villagers and gave their homes to us refugees. Some friends from my village and I were placed in a house high up in the Alps, about ten kilometers from Ratkersburg. Neta and her daughters lived about five kilometers away.

Naturally, the local people resented, even despised, us. As we'd feared the Soviet communists back home, we now lived in fear of partisan activity against us. Wild stories circulated. Local partisans wearing firemen badges had raped refugee women, plundered their homes, shot at young people. Living in fear, we kept our doors bolted. Women never traveled alone. Our young people kept a strict curfew.

By December 1944, the battlefront was once again too close for comfort. Searchlights fanned the night skies. Explosions rocked the windows as Russian bombs hit or missed their targets. Once more our whole community feared for our lives and thought about evacuation.

I received a letter from my sister Tina, who had fled to Germany. "Come to Germany," she wrote. "You'll be safer here."

Yes, I'll go. It's time to leave. So three weeks before Christmas, a friend named Anna and I hopped the milk truck down the mountain to town. We took a train to Graz, Austria, to apply for a visa to move to Germany.

It was toward evening before we started home. As the dark settled in, it started to rain. Anna fidgeted in her seat. "Miserable night to be out walking," she muttered.

I agreed.

She thought for a minute and then announced. "I'm going to get off before Ratkersburg and spend the night at my son's. You're welcome to come with me, Anna."

No. It didn't feel right. I didn't want to worry my housemates needlessly by changing my plans and not coming home.

The train slowed and my friend picked up her purse. "Coming?" she asked hopefully.

"Thank you, but I need to go home."

Once she'd waved good-bye and disappeared into the dusk and descending fog, I sat there alone, suddenly desolate and gripped by fear. As we passed through the next village, I pressed my face to the cold window. I could barely make out the rooftops. The rain turned to sleet, pecking at the window pane. *Anna, I should have gone with you*, I thought, as if I were a child separated from my mother and wishing her back to my side. *If only I weren't alone in the dark . . .*

About eight o'clock, I stepped off the train in Ratkersburg. Since morning an icy wind had come up and it tore through my threadbare coat. My thin kerchief seemed useless. The sleet stung my face. Seeking out the shelter of the dimly lit train station, I sat on a bench and deliberated about the walk ahead of me: at least an hour uphill, on a black, starless night. The footpath lay between a cemetery and vineyards and dense forest—and I'd have to ford a rushing stream.

As I thought about the dangers, a panic flooded my being. In the last twenty years I'd braced myself for dangers and journeys. But tonight my courage failed me. Utterly alone, far from home in a foreign land, the dam broke. *No way!* I thought. *There's no way I can make that trip tonight. In the pitch dark. In this weather.*

The train had pulled out, the last train of the night. I looked around the lonely station and timidly approached the stationmaster. "Sir, could I spend the night here, please?"

"No, ma'am," he said emphatically.

"I have so far to walk. . . ."

"Ma'am, I can't allow it," he said abruptly. He grabbed his coat and hat and fished for keys in his pocket. Then he headed for the door.

The panic mired my feet. *I can't go up that mountain.*

At the door the stationmaster grew downright impatient. "C'mon. I'm locking this place up." He must have read the alarm in my eyes. More kindly he added, "During an air raid, you'll be safer up the mountain anyway."

It seemed a small comfort. I listened to the receding crunch of his boots on gravel; the only man who could have helped me vanished into the icy mist.

For a few moments, I stood under the eaves of the straw roof. Finally I turned to the heavens, to the One my mother had turned to so often. "Father," I whispered, "I'm so scared. Take away this terror. Walk with me."

Suddenly there came a light, whiter than white and shining. It surrounded me.

Oh no, the bombers!

I scanned the sky for the telltale flares that preceded an air raid. I waited for the roar of planes, for the explosion of the hit.

Nothing. The sky was empty. Yet all around me the light shone. I felt as though I were standing in a dome, a huge globe of light about six feet across. Inside, it was bright as day. Outside, the night was black and strangely silent.

An indescribable peace suddenly filled my heart. I knew I could head toward the mountain. *I'll start out walking,* I thought with a robust confidence that I didn't have to force. With each step, the light moved with me, shining the path at my feet.

Instead of panic, joyous hymns welled up. "Oh, take my hand, my Father," I hummed softly, thinking it wise to stifle my strong urge to belt out the hymn tune with my lusty soprano.

As I started my ascent, the wind stopped, then the sleet. In fact, it grew warm as a summer's night. I loosed my kerchief. *How strange to be so warm in December.*

When I reached the dangerous stream, the water glistened like a thousand diamonds. I clearly saw the series of flat rocks scattered across the foaming water. Surefooted, I stepped from one to the next to the next until I reached the far bank.

The light guided and cheered me all the way up the mountain. As I neared the old house, I looked back over the treacherous pass. Like a ribbon of light, it lay behind me. Excitedly I knocked on the door, wanting to show my friends the awesome sight. The door opened. A strong gust of wind grabbed it, almost tearing it off its hinges. "Anna! Come in!" my friend yelled, pulling me inside. My housemates crowded around me. "Such a dreadful storm! Weren't you afraid?" one asked.

"No," I shook my head. "The storm died. . . ."

But I got no further. I suddenly could hear it too: the howling wind, the sleet pelting the windows, the moaning of the house.

While one friend busied herself with my supper, another took my coat. "It's dry," she said. Not quite believing what she was seeing, she repeated, "Anna, your coat's dry."

"I know," I said matter-of-factly.

I did my best to explain, but my friends looked at me with that puzzled expression I've come to expect. You see, from that night on I haven't known real fear, even in the succeeding months and years, when the pandemonium of the war—and the Cold War—separated me from my family.

For months I lived in a refugee camp in Munich, Germany. Then I went to Paraguay for nine years before coming to British Columbia in 1955. I was reunited with my three sisters, nieces and grandnieces—all had emigrated to western Canada.

In Paraguay I worked side by side with German Mennonite men, hacking out a place for our people in the dense jungle. Well into middle age, I carried buckets of damp earth away from a well-digging site. I cooked meals over primitive fires, feeding the men who built our houses. Eventually I owned a small hut with a straw roof—a home of my own. I lived alone, and at first I had no glass or wire netting to cover the windows, no lumber to build a proper door.

At times people warned me of thieves in the night or of poisonous snakes that would slither into open houses. Before December 1944 I would have been terrified. But no more. If fear drew near in the evenings, I'd start to sing, maybe "Oh, take my hand, my Father." Or I'd recite the poem I'd learned as a child: "Don't be afraid. God is here."

Don't be afraid. For fifty years it has been a theme of my life.

Don't be afraid. By the illuminating warmth of a kindly angelic light at Christmastime in wartorn Europe, it was God's word to me, a forty-year-old woman alone, afraid of the night.

GABRIEL'S LIGHT

ADAM DEMASI

My little brother Erik was the kind of kid who loved projects. He built elaborate models out of Legos and borrowed our father's tools to make forts in the woods behind our house. At Christmastime my parents and I watched him set off, dragging a saw half his size through the snow. Hours later he would reemerge, pulling the scrawniest pine tree along behind him. It was just like Erik to choose a tree nobody else wanted.

Putting up the tree had always been his responsibility. I didn't even know exactly where we kept the decorations, and I wasn't in the mood to sort through the boxes in the cluttered attic that day. I wasn't in the Christmas spirit at all. Four months earlier, Erik had died of a brain tumor. My parents kept telling me that Erik had gone to a better place, where God was watching over him, but I was bitter. Where was God when my twelve-year-old brother was dying? Why didn't God watch over him then?

I pulled down a box and untied the twine binding on the lid. A construction paper card slid out. Even in the dim light of the attic I recognized Erik's drawing style. On the outside of the card was a crayoned

Christmas tree topped with a star. Inside was a short inscription with two angels leaning over it, complete with yellow wings and halos. I brought the card to my parents.

"I've never seen this before," my mother said, passing the card over to my father. "Erik must have drawn these after he had his dream," he said.

"What dream?" I wanted to know. Mom ran her fingers over the card. "One night," she recalled, "when Erik was already very sick, he dreamed of angels. He said the angel Gabriel appeared at his bedside and cast a light, warm and bright, bright as Dad's blowtorch. The light made Erik feel well again."

"He asked us not to say anything about the dream," my father added, "but it was a comfort to him right up until the moment he died." I remembered that moment. We stood by Erik's bed when he turned his eyes to us and said, "I see the light again. I love you, Mommy and Daddy. I love you, Adam."

The light, I realized. Gabriel's light. Erik must have seen the angels again. God was right there, watching over.

That night, we propped Erik's crayon angels on the mantel and, as we dressed our store-bought tree with ornaments, the inscription on the Christmas card looked out on us:

To my family. Thank you for helping me through my difficult time.

Love, Eriky

I imagined my little brother among the bright angels in heaven, hard at work on his latest project. And Christmas felt a little more like Christmas again.

HOLIDAY CANDLES

BETTY GIRLING

The most memorable Christmas in my life occurred many years ago when I was eleven. My father and mother had left Ohio to homestead in Nebraska. Our first winter there began bleak and cold and, above all, lonely. We had no neighbors. Once there'd been other homesteaders nearby but they'd moved before we came. Across the fields their cabin stood empty.

In Ohio we'd been used to friends and activity and going to church, but here we lived too far out and my father made the long trip into town only occasionally for supplies.

A few days before Christmas, Pa saddled our horse, Thunder, and rode off to town to get the candles he'd promised for our tree.

Shortly after he left Mother and I were surprised to see a team of horses approaching the empty farmhouse across the field. Soon we could see figures unloading furniture.

"Neighbors!" Mother cried, joyfully.

The next moment she had on her coat and was trudging across our snow-crusted cornfields with a loaf of fresh baked bread. Soon Mother was back accompanied by a girl of my age.

"This is Sarah Goodman," she said.

Sarah and I looked at each other shyly. Then I found myself telling her all about the Christmas tree we were going to have when Pa got back from town.

Softly, Sarah said to me, "We're Jewish."

I'd never known a Jewish girl before. Suddenly I felt silly, babbling about trees and candles, and I was sorry for Sarah, not having any Christmas.

"Well, never mind," I told her, struck by a sudden thought, "you have special holidays too, I guess."

"Oh yes, we have Hanukkah," she began eagerly. "That's our Feast of Lights . . ." she broke off and jumped to her feet. "Oh, with all the moving, we've forgotten! Why it's already . . ." she counted on her fingers, "it's the fifth day. And I don't even know where we packed the menorah!" Then with a hasty good-bye she ran out and across the fields to her own house.

Mother and I watched her go in surprise, wondering what a "menorah" might be. Even as we watched it began to snow.

I stayed at the window all afternoon, peering into the white maelstrom. Faster and thicker the snow fell—till I couldn't see Mother's lilac bush a scarce five feet away.

At six Pa had not returned and Mother's face was grim. Here on the plains blizzard is a fearsome word. Hadn't they told us in town about the homesteader they found last winter, frozen to death only four feet from his own barn door?

At eleven, when Mother finally put me to bed, the blizzard was still raging and Pa had not returned.

At dawn the storm was over. Deep snowdrifts piled high around the house, but the sky was clearing. Mother was sitting in a chair, still waiting.

Suddenly we heard shouts and we raced to the door.

Pushing through the drifts came Father, Sarah Goodman and her parents. In they tramped. Soon we were all clustered around the kitchen stove, getting warm.

"It was a miracle," Pa said. "That's what it was, a miracle!"

While mother cooked breakfast Pa told us how he'd got lost in the storm. The road was completely obliterated, he could see nothing in the dark, and had to depend on the horse's instinct for guidance. But finally Thunder wouldn't go on.

"I was nearly frozen by then," Pa said. "So I jumped off the horse and started leading him, just to keep warm. For hours we floundered on. We'd work one way till the drifts got too deep, then turn and work another."

Pa knew he was pretty close to exhaustion when suddenly, through the swirling snow off to one side, he saw some tiny pinpoints of light.

"As I led Thunder toward those lights, I prayed they would still keep shining, and when I reached them I found myself at the Goodmans' cabin. There in the window was a great candlestick, like none I'd ever seen before. Nine candles it held, six of them lighted."

"That was our menorah," said Sarah, "for Hanukkah, our Feast of Lights. I put it in the window."

"Then you saved Pa's life!"

"Not exactly," said Mr. Goodman, gently. "Sarah really put it on the window sill hoping you would see it and know that she was celebrating her holiday, at this time, like you will be keeping your Christmas."

Mother set us down to breakfast just then and Pa bowed his head, saying, "Almighty God, we thank thee for the blessings of this season."

"MAYBE IT WAS A CHRISTMAS ANGEL"

JOAN WESTER ANDERSON

It was a few days before Christmas in Hamilton, Indiana. Ten-year-old Kari had gone with her baby sister Amy and her mom on some errands, and now they were buying a few things at the grocery store. Kari was a bit tired. She would rather have stayed at home, but her mom needed her to help watch Amy.

Finally, they unloaded their items at the checkout counter. Kari looked idly around, then noticed a plastic mayonnaise jar on a shelf near the cash register. A picture of a girl was taped on it, and below that was a handwritten sign that read "Beth L. has cancer, desperately needs donations for bone marrow transplant."

Why, Kari realized she *knew* Beth. Beth was in a higher grade at her school. But Kari hadn't known Beth was sick.

"Look, Mom." Kari pointed at the empty jar. "I know this girl."

Her mother read the sign, and her eyes filled with tears. "That poor family—they must be so worried," she murmured.

"Could we give them some money?" Kari asked. Then she remembered with dismay how tight their own budget was. There was no way

Mom could spare anything, especially right now, the week before Christmas.

But Mom had just been handed several bills in change. She looked at the money for a moment, then put it all in the jar. "This is all I have," she said sadly. "I wish it were more."

Kari knew the donation was a real sacrifice. As they walked to the car she felt tears spring to her eyes. She was proud of what her mom had done.

Mom started the engine and pulled out of the parking lot. As the car headed down a dark highway, Kari closed her eyes tightly and prayed for Beth. What must it be like, having cancer and being scared?

Then Kari heard something hit the windshield. It sounded like a pebble. "Look at that!" her mother cried.

Kari's eyes popped open. A small ball of light, shining a bright silver blue, was bouncing on the outside of the front window. And then, unbelievably, it was *inside* the car, flashing and shining, getting bigger and bigger, wrapping them all in a brilliant cocoon.

Kari was astonished. The light couldn't be coming from outside, she realized; theirs was the only car on the dark road, and there were no streetlights along their route, and not even any Christmas lights. Besides, the ball was far too bright to be just a reflection. Awed, Kari watched it. It was dazzling, radiant, yet somehow joyful, too, as if . . . as if it were *dancing*. And was that the outline of a figure in its center? Kari couldn't tell for sure.

She looked outside and noticed that the whole area where they were riding seemed to be illuminated. She looked at Amy. The toddler's eyes were wide in wonder.

As quickly as the light had appeared, it vanished, and the interior of the car was completely dark again. By now Kari's mother had pulled off the road, and she turned to Kari. "You look as shocked as I am," she said. "What did you see?"

"A ball of light! It came inside the car!" Kari cried. "Mom, what was it?"

"I don't know," her mother said slowly, thoughtfully. "Maybe it was a Christmas angel, bringing us a message of hope for Beth, or thanking us for our money to her. . . ."

Kari thought about it. "Do angels do that? Do they bring good news to ordinary people like us?"

"They did on the first Christmas," her mother reminded her, smiling. "Why not now?"

The strange light didn't return. But this Christmas turned out to be the best one Kari's family had ever had. Even though they didn't have much money, they felt very blessed, as if the joy of the bouncing spark was still in their midst.

And when vacation ended, Kari received another gift. "How is Beth?" she asked a friend on their first day back in school.

"Oh, Beth had her transplant and she's able to come back to school today," her friend replied.

Kari was surprised and happy. She knew that not every sick person got well, especially not right away. Sometimes things like this took time, because God's plan wasn't the same for everyone.

But no matter what the results seemed to be, God *always* wanted His people to care for each other and to offer their help, even when it wasn't easy, even when it cost time or money. That was the best way to make earth more like heaven, to make every day like Christmas.

An angel of light had told Kari so.

CHAPTER TWO

WHISPERING HOPE

The hopes and fears of all the years
Are met in thee tonight.

What do hope and fear have in common? They are both emotions that bring the future into the present. We hope for the best. We fear the worst.

Even at the Christmas season it is easy to dwell on the negative. We may be like heartbroken Louise Tucker Jones. Dreading the holiday at the beginning of her story, "Christmas Promise," she prayed, "Dear God, Christmas is for children, not for me anymore." But the child born in Bethlehem came to us with the promise of hope. In I Timothy 1:1, the apostle Paul actually called Jesus "our hope."

The stories in this section are "quiet" stories, in which God's messengers whisper, "God has not forgotten you. He is with you today, and He will be with you tomorrow." Emily Dickinson called hope "the thing with feathers," like a bird—or maybe an angel—that sings a soft melody without words. It's the song Louise Tucker Jones heard in her spirit on Christmas morning: "the promise of a brighter tomorrow."

—E.B.

CHRISTMAS PROMISE

LOUISE TUCKER JONES

My family had a longtime tradition of gathering on Christmas Eve in my parents' home in Henryetta, Oklahoma. In 1972, my husband Carl and I lived about an hour away in a little town outside Tulsa. Our son Aaron was four that year, and he was used to waking up on Christmas morning in his grandparents' house. "Santa knows where I am," he declared, his eyes bright. "Just like God does," I used to tell him. Every December 24, Carl and I loaded the car with gifts and homemade goodies, and then the three of us hit the road, singing carols along the way.

But there was no singing in our house in 1972. Just thinking about Christmas was hard, not to mention shopping, decorating, baking and pretending to enjoy the holiday. Our three-month-old son Travis had died from heart failure that summer, and I felt like part of me had died with him. Only Aaron kept me going. Much as he missed his baby brother, he was still a child, with a child's expectations for a brighter tomorrow.

I had hoped to make the holiday as normal as possible for Aaron, but in spite of my good intentions, I wanted to turn right around at my parents' front door. They had outdone themselves with festive trimmings, and the sight of it all overwhelmed me. "The tree I cut this year was so big," Daddy said proudly, "I had to chop four feet off the top."

I managed a smile, but there was no joy in my heart. My sister and brothers tried putting on brave faces, but sorrow hung in the air because of what had happened to Carl and me. Each gift I wrapped for one of the other kids, I remembered the toys I'd bought for Travis that would never find their way under the tree. *Dear God*, I prayed, *Christmas is for children, not for me anymore.*

Relatives started dropping in, and my parents' small house began to bulge at the seams. Soon there was so much noise and laughter I wanted to scream. "Carl?" I called, desperate. I searched through the crowd until I spotted him. Hurrying over, I grabbed his arm and dragged him out to the backyard. "I can't do this," I whispered. "I don't want to stay." Carl led me to the quiet of our car, and we climbed inside. For a while we sat there saying nothing.

Then Carl had an idea: "Dad's house." His dad had remarried after being a widower for several years and was spending the holidays with his new wife's family. We called, and he encouraged us to make use of his home, only fifteen minutes away. It sounded good to us, but there was a big problem for Aaron. "Santa won't be able to find me!" he said.

"He knows where you are," I assured him. "Just like God." But I knew how Aaron felt. I was afraid my grief had pushed me to a place where God's love couldn't find me. We grabbed a few things we'd need overnight and explained to the family that we'd return on Christmas Day.

Aaron dropped off to sleep the minute I tucked him in at Pa-Pa's. Carl dragged in the chopped-off treetop he'd sneaked into the car trunk before we left my parents' house. We found an old tree stand in the attic and set the tree up in the living room. It stood there looking totally forlorn in front of the dark window.

"Now what?" I asked. Carl and I giggled like children as we came up with ideas for decorations. We popped popcorn and strung it. I made chains from ribbon and tied bows on the branches. We found a drawer filled with tiny plastic cups, which we covered with aluminum foil and topped with curly ribbon. They looked like shiny little bells hanging on the tree. We spread a white sheet underneath and decorated it with wrapped packages. Aaron's Santa present was displayed in front—the complete set of dinosaurs he'd been asking for all year. The result looked like an honest-to-goodness Christmas tree.

"Almost perfect," I said. "If only I knew how to make an angel for the top!"

"Santa really did know where I was!" Aaron cried the next morning. "And he brought my dinosaurs!" I hadn't seen him so happy in a long while. Carl slipped his arm around my waist. And at that moment I felt joy for the first time since we'd lost our son. God's love had reached past my sadness and found me again. Despite all that had happened, it really was Christmas. This was Christmas as it should be, filled with the surprises and pleasures of childhood, and the promise of a brighter tomorrow. I looked at our tree by the window, and I could almost see an angel shining at the top.

"DO YOU WANT HELP?"

JOHN POWERS

No matter which direction I walked on the night of December 23, 1972, the sleet found a place to stick to my blue uniform. It was the type of night a foot patrolman wonders why he became a cop. I was doing security checks in an industrial park in South Jamaica, Queens, New York. Every business in this remote area had been closed for hours, and there wasn't another human being for blocks as I made my rounds throughout the eerily quiet complex.

By 9:00 P.M. the wind and frigid weather had intensified, and I took shelter under a large canopy, clicking my heels together to get the blood moving in my feet. Finally my sergeant came by and told me to stay where I was until my shift was over. As the squad car pulled off I felt uneasy about being alone in such a deserted place. *Stay alert, Powers*, I told myself. *Don't get spooked.* Then I heard footsteps. I braced my hand on the gun in my holster, and swung around at the ready.

"Sorry, officer, I didn't mean to startle you."

White male, fair-skinned, five feet ten inches, 170 pounds, I noted, my training kicking in. Late fifties, early sixties, wears his age well.

"The name's Ed."

I removed my hand from my gun. "Officer Powers," I introduced myself, deciding the guy was harmless. "I'm on patrol."

Ed said his sympathy went out to me, working outdoors in this weather. "And at Christmastime, no less," he said. "There was a time in my life when I was caught out in the cold. It was a night very similar to this."

I could tell this was the beginning of a long story, and that this guy was going to talk until he finished telling it, but I was glad to have the company and settled in to listen.

"Thirty-five years ago, on Christmas Eve morning," Ed began, "I crawled out of the cardboard box I called home on the Bowery. Hung over and half frozen, I looked up through the falling snow at the Manhattan Bridge, hanging in midair like a ghost. By the time I hit Canal Street, I was shivering, my mind slipping in and out of focus. But I had plans: This would be the day I was going to end my life. The looming iron ghost was the answer. I would jump in front of a truck coming off the bridge. A semi-trailer, I thought, that will do the job."

So on Christmas Eve 1937, in the depths of alcoholic despair, Ed waited at the foot of the Manhattan Bridge. The only thing keeping him standing was knowing that any minute his misery would be over. During the several hours he stood there, however, not a single truck came off that bridge.

"When I could no longer bear my hunger, I decided to try my luck at panhandling—for old-time's sake." Ed grinned.

Back on Canal Street the first person he asked turned away disgusted. The next person he asked was a distinguished-looking young man of thirty or so. He wore a lovely tan overcoat, dress shoes and no hat (which Ed thought odd). "Sir, could you help me get a cup of coffee?" Ed asked.

The young man glanced around. "Follow me," he said, gesturing toward a diner. There he invited Ed to take a seat at the counter and ordered him coffee and a deluxe breakfast. "A meal I'll never forget," Ed said. Before paying the bill, the young man asked the waitress to add a hot roast beef sandwich and coffee to go. Ed was amazed by the stranger's generosity, and for a time he was distracted from his desperate plan. "A warm lunch tucked into my coat pocket," Ed said, "I went back to the alley where I'd spent the night, dozed for a while, then ate when I awoke. My stomach was full, but my situation was still bleak. What did I have to live for? Determined to see my plan through, I returned to the bridge."

Ed waited again, until afternoon became evening. Still not a truck in sight. "God, I do not want to live another night. Please help me," he prayed, not knowing the bridge had been closed to truck traffic due to fierce weather conditions.

Maybe because it was the only thing he knew how to do, maybe out of habit, Ed went back to panhandling on Canal Street. The few people he came across had their own challenges in this brutal weather, trying to get home to their families for Christmas Eve.

In his stupor Ed at first didn't recognize one of the people he approached: "The young man looked me in the eye and said, 'Do you want help?' At that moment I felt a blazing warmth throughout my body. Something in my life had changed."

Once again the young man led Ed into the diner they had visited that morning. He ordered a hot open-faced turkey sandwich and all the traditional holiday side dishes.

While Ed ate, the young man excused himself, returning to the diner in about fifteen minutes without a hint that he'd been out in the storm. In fact, Ed never noticed a single flake or wet spot marring the dapper tan overcoat or fancy dress shoes.

"We must hurry," the young man said, putting away his wallet and jostling Ed out the door. "We have an appointment with a friend of mine."

The young man led Ed at a fast pace to a building a few blocks away, where a sign advertised Day Employment. Inside, the young man's friend said a two-week job was available, if Ed was interested, for a watchman at a warehouse in Queens. Ed nodded at the young man, who said to his friend, "Make the arrangements. We'll be right back."

Now the young man hurried Ed to an Army-Navy store, where he consulted Ed about his size and bought a warm winter jacket, two sets of khaki pants and shirts, work boots, underwear, long johns, socks and a woolen watch cap. Ed was flabbergasted and somewhat embarrassed as they rushed back to the employment office with the packages. "Right in the bathroom of the employment agency I put on a complete new outfit from head to toe," Ed said. "Wonderful, warm, dry clothes."

Before leaving the building, the young man gave Ed subway and bus directions to the Queens warehouse—and a five-dollar bill. Finally Ed asked his name: Jim. "How will I ever repay you, Jim?" Ed wanted to know.

The young man put his hand on Ed's shoulder. "If you stay off the street and don't abuse your body with liquor, that will be my payment."

Together they walked to the subway station, where the two men parted ways. "Merry Christmas," Jim said. Ed waved good-bye as he descended the stairs with his packages.

After an hour-and-a-half trip, Ed arrived at the warehouse in Queens, where he found the owner's son, Phil, waiting for him with open arms. "My whole family is grateful to have you here," Phil said. They went over the arrangement—two weeks at the warehouse day and night, a cot to sleep on and takeout food nearby. After giving Ed a few more instructions and an advance in salary, Phil was on his way.

"And that's how I came to be in my own warehouse," Ed explained, "secure and warm on Christmas Eve, when only a few hours earlier I wanted the final curtain to ring down. I owed my life to Jim, and I thanked God for putting him in my path, not once but twice."

Ed didn't think he could be any happier. But then on Christmas Day a car pulled up at the warehouse, and in walked Phil and his family. Phil introduced his wife and their two daughters, who set up a turkey dinner with all the trimmings for Ed. Then they handed him a present wrapped in holiday paper. When Ed opened it and found a beautiful brown cable-knit sweater, he put it to his face to smell the freshness of the wool. He couldn't believe his good fortune.

During his two-week stint, Ed made a point of getting to know all the employees. When Phil offered him the job full-time, Ed jumped at the chance. "It's settled, then," Phil said. "Follow me." And they walked to a plywood-framed structure at the rear of the plant.

Here in the story, Ed stopped abruptly. "Why, pardon me, Officer Powers," he said, "you've been in the cold long enough." I'd honestly forgotten about the weather, and the time, and a glance at my watch verified that my shift was over. "Step inside for just a moment," Ed said. "It will be the perfect end to my story."

I followed Ed to the plywood structure, just as he had followed Phil some thirty-five years before. Ed opened the door and the lights went on.

"Come in, come in," he said. And I entered a comfortable three-room apartment, complete with all the amenities and wallpapered to match the decor. "I've lived here ever since," Ed explained. "The owner's family and the employees never forget me on a holiday, and they always remember that I consider Christmas Eve my birthday, the day Jim saved my life and I was reborn.

"One more thing," Ed said. "I eventually sent some money to Jim, in care of his friend at the agency. I wanted him to know how well things had turned out for me. But the money came back with a note. A man at the agency remembered me well, but he knew of no Jim. You see, no one had been with me at the agency that Christmas Eve. No one visible, that is."

I left Ed with a new spring in my step. His story carried me through many a hard tour on the force. I had met someone whose life was completely changed, thanks to the goodness in this world, and to God's abundant goodness, which rains on us from heaven.

A ROSE FOR AMY

SARAH AMES

There's a framed picture in my house of a brown-haired girl I never knew, but she has been part of my life for as long as I can remember. My dad is a real storyteller, and he's always entertaining us with his "little boy in Iowa" memories. His particular favorites are about his sister Amy. My dad had two older brothers and two younger sisters, but he was especially close to Amy. "Everybody loved Amy," Dad said. Growing up, listening to his many stories, I began to love her too. Now I feel close to her in a way I could never have imagined.

When she was a high school student, just as I am now, Amy was diagnosed with Hodgkin's lymphoma, stage two. She fought the disease, staying in school and playing softball. "She was getting good at it," Dad remembers. But Amy lost her struggle with cancer when she was eighteen.

The story became more real to me five years ago when I was diagnosed with Hodgkin's lymphoma, stage two, just like my aunt Amy. It started with swollen glands, and then I was itching with what I thought were bug bites. The school nurse practitioner said it was something that had to be looked at. I had a slew of tests that fall of seventh grade, and I started chemotherapy. But somehow I wasn't worried. *God is with me*, I thought, and I believed it. "Everything will be all right," I said whenever anyone looked glum. I was determined to stay in school, and I was looking forward to our Christmas concert at church. I was playing the organ for the children's choir, and the concert was so important we started practicing in October.

Then in December I developed a blood clot and had to be taken to the hospital. The doctors didn't know how long I'd have to stay. For the first time, I worried. Really worried. Worse, I was afraid. *What's happening to me?* I wondered. Sometimes I lay in bed too scared to fall asleep, scared I wouldn't wake up. Two long weeks passed. The hospital was an hour from home, but my parents came to see me every night, even though they both worked and took care of my two younger brothers. They tried to cheer me up, but one night I burrowed into Dad's arms, shaking with fear. "I don't know what to do," I whispered. "God isn't with me anymore."

Dad brushed my hair back from my face and looked deep into my eyes. "How about your favorite story?" he asked. Dad and his stories . . . but I listened, wanting to hear this one again. When I was little, my favorite story about my aunt Amy involved Saint Thérèse, a young nun in nineteenth-century France, who's called the Little Flower. "Amy was in a coma in the hospital, remember?" Dad said. Dad's parents asked God to allow Amy to go home just one more time, and they implored in Saint Thérèse's name. Tradition says that if your prayers are granted, you will receive a white rose as a sign from Saint Thérèse. "I remember," I said to Dad. "Amy got better, and you found a single white rose in her room." "Yes," he said quietly. "She came home with us for three months."

I desperately wanted to go home too. Days and days went by, and I wasn't even halfway through my treatment. I began to think I'd never leave the hospital. I missed the school pageant, and worst of all, I missed the Christmas concert at my church. The day after the concert was the darkest day of my life. By nighttime, I didn't think I could take it anymore. I paced around my room, hating the hospital—angry with the doctors, the nurses, even with God. That's when the door opened and Mom peeked in. "Someone to see you," she said.

Mom led me down the hall to the waiting room. I turned the corner and spotted two boys from my children's choir. "They insisted on coming to see you," said their mother. One of the boys stepped forward, one arm hidden behind him. "We wanted to be sure you're okay," he said. Bringing his arm around from behind his back, he presented me with a gift, a single white rose.

I had to catch my breath. How could I have ever been so full of fear and anger? In front of me was proof of God's love, shining from those two boys' cherubic faces. He was with me just as He had been with my aunt Amy. It was disappointing that I didn't make the Christmas concert, but I knew I'd be there for the next one.

THE BOY AND THE CRÈCHE

CLARKE K. OLER

There he was again! He was barely six years old and wearing his red knit stocking hat, his face pressed against the iron fence that surrounded the garden of the Church of the Holy Trinity in New York City. It was not usual for a child so young to be out on the streets alone, and I had seen this boy before. He always wore the same grimy red hat pulled over his ears, the same old sneakers, the same tattered jacket. Several times I had spoken to him, trying to find out who he was, but each time he had just looked at me with large solemn eyes that, together with his small grim mouth, conveyed a smoldering distrust. Without a word he would run off down the street and disappear.

It was Christmas Eve 1967. The snow had been falling all day, and I was looking out a second-floor window of the rectory, calculating how much snow the sexton and I would have to shovel before the people started arriving in three hours for the midnight service.

Eighty-eighth Street was deserted, the pedestrians having settled in at home for the night. The church garden was dark, and a single street lamp poked feeble beams through the foggy night that reflected off the great glistening Gothic gateposts now sporting white tam-o'-shanters of snow.

The brightest light on the street shone from inside the large crèche in the church garden. Realistic beams and cobwebs were painted on the plywood stable that housed nearly life-sized figures of the Holy Family. Joseph stood beside seated Mary, who gazed lovingly at the baby Jesus in the wooden crib. A shepherd held a plaster lamb in his arms, and three elegant kings bearing gifts knelt before the manger. The ground surrounding the wooden manger was covered with a thick carpet of real straw, a gift from the mounted police in Central Park who delivered several bales faithfully every year. The Christmas crèche was a well-known feature in the neighborhood.

Then I saw him again. The little boy, with that unmistakable red hat pulled down over his ears. He was peering through the fence at the crèche. As I watched, he ventured timidly through the church gate and across the fresh snow. For a moment he stood before the crèche. Then he climbed inside and lay on his back in the straw. Every now and then someone would pass by on the street, but no one noticed the little boy curled up under the gentle gaze of the Virgin Mary.

I could see the top of his red cap. Once, then again and again, when the street was empty, he reached up. I saw his small fingers softly touch the cheek of the Virgin. For fifteen minutes I watched, not daring to go outside because I knew the moment I opened the door he would scamper away. Then all of a sudden something startled him. In an instant he was up and running across the snow and out the gate. He disappeared into the night.

I never saw him again. But every Christmas I think of him. I remember how I held my breath that night, knowing there was nothing I could do that wouldn't frighten him away, hoping, praying that the Blessed

Mother would convey to him something of the peace and hope for which he was reaching when he touched the cheek of her image. Could a crèche figure be an angel of peace and hope for a lonely boy?

Though I could do nothing for him that night, he did something for me. He reminded me that in my heart, in every heart, there is a longing, an ache that doesn't go away. And so we reach up to touch the face of God to receive His inexpressible blessing. In mysterious ways, especially on Christmas Eve, He gives His gift, and bids us to watch for the lonely ones who need our touch and love throughout the year.

A CHRISTMAS TAIL

CAREY MOORE

I f I were to have a white—happy—Christmas that year, it would be only in my dreams. More fitting to my prospects were the sentiments expressed in the old carol, "In the bleak midwinter . . ." Or, perhaps more apt, "I'll have a blue, blue Christmas."

Christmas 1983 found me alone, living in a rented room, the New Jersey winter howling outside. An hour away, my children—two teen-aged sons and two daughters—lived in a charming but sagging house with their mother. It was the darkest period of my life. I deeply regretted the break-up of our family.

I had been fortunate to find a room in a large house where the family welcomed boarders. I, the only renter at the time, could eat in the kitchen nook, store food in the fridge and do my laundry in the family washing machine. Occasionally I was included in the family evening meal—the family being the mother and two young-adult children.

It was Christmas Eve, and a place was set for me at the dinner table. The usual family number was augmented that evening by the arrival of a second daughter and a couple of young friends. Dinner conversation was lively with rapid repartee, interesting stories and frequent laughter that

went well with the succulent pork roast and fresh vegetables. There was also an air of excitement about the place, such as is occasioned by a secret being kept—to be revealed on Christmas morning. It concerned the younger daughter. And, in a way, it concerned me.

Yet, as I sat and listened to my dinner companions, my woeful thoughts kept going back to my kids. Christmas Day I would probably get to see only my daughters—and only for a short while. Nor could I "treat" them this Christmas; though I was now employed with a publishing firm as a book editor, I'd been out of work for a year, and I didn't have ten dollars to spare. I'd be lucky if my '74 Buick would get me to the family home safely.

Nevertheless, the "secret" had momentarily relieved my sadness. The kitten-gift would not be revealed until Christmas morning. Where would the kitten sleep on Christmas Eve? There was only one "off-limits" place in the house—my room. So I was asked to "put up" the kitty—nicknamed "O.J." because of its orange and white stripy coloring—and I agreed.

Following supper, I excused myself and retreated upstairs to the quiet. At the top of the stairs, I noticed my bedroom door was closed, when I knew I had left it open. Upon entering the room, I discovered, in a corner behind the door, a small cage that held O.J. Instinctively, I opened the door of the cage and a sweet kitten walked out. For some time, she went about the room, checking its nooks and corners, and then jumped into my lap. I petted her for a while until she hopped down and disappeared under my bed. Then I became preoccupied with something and more or less forgot my quiet guest. After I turned out the light and lay down, sleep came quickly.

In the middle of the night I was awakened. The house was quiet, dark. Something soft on my face had brought me to consciousness.

Gradually, I realized that O.J. was lying on my pillow and placing her little front paws, one after the other, on my face. It was a lovely feeling, her "marching" on my cheeks and forehead. For some time, she lay there, patting my face with her paws, as if with a loving caress. For what seemed like a long time, it was just O.J. and me. She purred intermittently and kept up her "march" on my face.

Suddenly, I was moved, touched. I was not alone. Christmas had come and found me receiving love. Tears came to my eyes, tears of joy and gratitude for God's message: He had not forgotten me. In His wise providence, that Christmas, I had my own night visitor. It was as though an angel had come to me and whispered, "It's all right. Keep your hopes up. I'm here with you."

Next morning, O.J. found a loving home in the arms of a very surprised and happy girl. And that day I looked in wonder at this small "night visitor" who had brought Christmas near. With the warmth of knowing that the heavenly Father loved me, I didn't have a blue Christmas after all. Down inside, I had a hopeful joy.

Though my wife and I were divorced within the year, my "life" did not end. In middle age I returned to school to get a second master's degree, changing careers, from book editor to librarian. Through mutual friends I met a wonderful woman, Pam Rosewell, whom I married in 1986. Though we've never had a cat, we welcome two dogs as part of our household, now deep in the heart of Texas. This past Christmas we put extra leaves in the table when my two grown sons came, and during the day both of my daughters called long distance for prolonged chats with all the family members. It was one of the brightest days and most joyous of Christmases of my life.

CHAPTER THREE

WATCHING
WITH LOVE

For Christ is born of Mary;
And gathered all above,
While mortals sleep, the angels keep
Their watch of wondering love.

K eeping watch." It's a phrase we connect with the biblical Christmas story. The King James Version of Luke describes shepherds keeping watch over their flocks by night. If I were writing a Christmas song, I might think of a *mother* keeping a loving watch over a baby—Mary and her holy child, lain in manger hay. But here in his Bethlehem carol, Phillips Brooks describes angels gathered above the stable birth scene, keeping a "watch of wondering love."

Three dramatic stories in this section tell of protection and intervention in life-threatening situations; Karen Tribble, Ron Gullion and Eric Lenihan encounter the physical power of their heavenly watchers. Kym Coleman's story is more low-key. She senses someone was watching out for her well-being. Why? Because "it's Christmas."

— E.B.

STORMY WEATHER

KAREN TRIBBLE

Christmas Eve and I had one last-minute errand. I'd already bought four-year-old Emily the Spirograph she'd wanted. And for Lindsey, six, who was really into New Kids on the Block, I'd gotten a New Kids doll. We'd decorated the tree, made cookies. All I had left to do was get some fresh fruit for their stockings. Steeling myself, I called my ex-husband. "Can you take the girls this afternoon? I have a last-minute Santa trip to make.

"Just do me a favor," I added. "Don't let them open presents yet." The girls would be spending the week after Christmas with him. They could open their presents then. I didn't want him to spoil what little I could afford to give. He'd already spoiled everything else, as far as I was concerned, when he'd left me and demanded a divorce.

I dropped off Emily and Lindsey, and when they returned a couple hours later they were on cloud nine. "Look what Santa brought me at Daddy's," Emily burst out. "A Spirograph!" "And, Mom, look!" Lindsey said. "A New Kids doll." If their father had been there I would have exploded. He'd betrayed me—again. *Don't ruin Christmas for the girls*, I reminded myself. *This is their first year without all of us together. Don't make it any worse.*

"That's wonderful," I said. "I hope Santa doesn't get confused when

he visits here." I dreaded the girls' disappointment the next morning when they'd get the same presents.

At bedtime I listened to their prayers and told them the story of the first Christmas. "The angels are looking down on you just as they looked down on the Baby Jesus when he was born in that stable," I finished.

The morning dawned gray and cold. Inside, the girls opened their few packages. "Mom!" Emily cried. "Another Spirograph so my friend can play with one." "Look," said Lindsey, "my New Kids doll has a twin!" They were even thrilled with the fruit in their stockings. The answering machine clicked on, but I ignored it. Probably their dad calling, and I couldn't bear to hear his voice. *If I live to be a hundred, my anger at him will never subside.* I cooked a big breakfast, then dressed the girls in their best outfits for the trip to Louisville to see their grandparents and cousins.

The ugly weather didn't concern me. Louisville was only two hours away, and it was a trip I'd made countless times. But halfway there the rain really came down. It turned to sleet, and the roads became slick. I passed cars that had spun off the interstate. The surface was covered with ice. But it was too late to turn back. I would only be following the storm instead of escaping it. The only choice was to move ahead cautiously.

Then we came to the crest of a hill. Ahead there must have been two dozen cars stopped in the middle of the road, turned every which way as though they had been spun like tops. I pumped the brakes, keeping the steering wheel straight. "God, you'll have to help me." Miraculously, we slid to a stop—only inches from the car in front of us. But we weren't safe there! Any car coming over that hill was a threat with that ice. We would be the first ones hit! There were cars on either side. I couldn't move. I reached for Emily and Lindsey's hands in the seat next to me.

"Girls, remember what I said about Christmas being Jesus' birthday and how the angels were there with him in the stable when he was born? Well, we have to believe they're here with us right now. We need their help.

"Dear Jesus," I prayed, "we have weathered a tough storm this last year, and I know we're going to come out of it just fine." I could see that now. "Please help us get through this storm and safely to Grandma's house."

"Amen," the girls said.

In the rearview mirror I watched a van crest the hill and come barreling down toward us. *Please, don't let us be hit.* I reached my arms around my daughters and braced myself for the crunch of metal. But the van sailed over the car next to us, as though it took an invisible ramp on the interstate. As it hit the ground in a vacant spot, I noticed that a path had cleared before us. I inched ahead, zigzagging between the twisted cars. None of them seemed badly damaged. They just couldn't get traction on the icy highway. "Thank you, God," I prayed. "Thank you, Jesus."

As we finally pulled onto a long clear stretch of the interstate, Emily asked, "Mommy, did you see the angels?"

Goose bumps shivered down my arm. "Where, dear?"

"All around our car after we prayed." I didn't doubt it for a moment.

When we finally reached my parents' house, all in one piece, I told my relatives about our near disaster. As the adults talked, the little ones opened their presents. Wrapping paper flew, and more exclamations came. "Mom, look what I got!" Another Spirograph? Or a New Kids on the Block doll? It wouldn't have mattered. My anger at their father seemed less important now too. We were safe and blessed and watched over. That's what counted. "This is the best Christmas ever," Emily said.

"Yes," added Lindsey. "And we got to do it three times!"

A GIANT BESIDE
OUR HOUSE

RON GULLION

I'*m in our yard on Big Fir Court, gazing up at the mighty 250-foot tree the street is named for. Rising from the corner of our property to the height of a twenty-story building, the great white fir dwarfs our home and everything in sight like some ancient giant. It gives the illusion of leaning ominously toward me, creaking and swaying ever so slightly in the rustling wind.*

Look! It's not leaning, it's falling! It's toppling toward our house, gaining momentum, rushing to meet its shadow, until finally it crumples the roof and splinters through the living room and front bedroom with a sickening, thunderous roar. I let out a cry. Alison's room!

I awoke in a drenching sweat and sat straight up trying to blink away the terrifying vision. Another nightmare. I slipped out of bed and stole a peek into Alison's room. Our nine-year-old daughter was sleeping peacefully, as was eleven-year-old Heath across the hall. But I couldn't shake the irrational fear until I'd checked. This was not the first time I'd dreamed of such an accident. In another dream I'd seen a giant tree limb tearing loose and slamming down on Heath, leaving him crippled.

As a computer engineer, I deal with quantifiable information. I don't

pay much attention to impractical things like dreams. But these nightmares were so vivid and frightening. I eased back into bed next to my wife Nita, but not before looking out the window at the tree. There it stood, stately and still, its coarse bark ghostly pale in the faint moonlight.

A few nights later I had another dream, this one more puzzling than alarming:

I am in our yard and in front of me stands a white angel. The angel has a broken wing.

What did all these dreams mean?

Then one day I noticed a twenty-foot dead limb dangling from the fir. Out here in the Northwest we call a dangerous limb like that a widow maker. I remembered the dream about Heath. "Don't go near that tree," I warned him. That Saturday I enlisted a neighbor to help me rope it down; all week I'd worried about the precarious branch. Later I had some other dead limbs removed too.

Why am I so concerned about this tree? I wondered. It's stood here for generations. It even survived the fierce Columbus Day storm of '62.

My nightmares about the tree eventually subsided. Christmas season arrived and Nita and I rushed madly to get our shopping done. More than anything, Alison wanted a Cabbage Patch doll. We scoured the stores around Portland with no luck. Everywhere we went it was the same story. "Sorry, folks," said the clerk inevitably. "We sold out our Cabbage Patch dolls weeks ago."

Finally Nita settled on a handmade rag doll. It was thicker and heavier than the Cabbage Patch version, but there was something about it that caught our fancy. "Well," sighed Nita as we paid for it, "this will have to do."

"Alison will love it," I reassured her.

We arrived home to a surprise. Alison had impetuously decided to rearrange her room. She'd been talking about it for days, but Nita had implored her to wait until the holiday excitement died down. "Then I'll help you," she'd promised.

Instead Alison had recruited her brother for the task, getting Heath to help drag her heavy bed across the room. "I just wanted to get it done now, Mommy," she explained as Nita surveyed the scene with obvious displeasure. "It's important." Alison's toys and furniture spilled out into the hall. By bedtime, however, Alison had her room in order again and we could scarcely hide our admiration.

"See?" said Alison knowingly. "It's not such a big deal."

Outside I heard the wind whistle through the big fir.

A howling blizzard marked Christmas Eve. I drove home from work through swirling snow and pounding winds. I pulled into the driveway, turned up my collar and hurried inside to get ready for church. Church was not one of my priorities even under the best circumstances, and on a night like this I didn't want to be anywhere but inside my house, Christmas Eve or not. But I'd promised.

At the service with Nita and the kids, I felt strangely detached as I hunched in the pew with my arms folded tightly, thinking about whether I even believed that God was a part of my life. I'd been raised in church but that was a long time ago. Now I certainly didn't feel any "tidings of comfort and joy." God may have created the world and all its wonders, but I didn't see where that had much to do with my life. If God was real, He was much too remote for me to have faith in.

We arrived home late, and the wind and snow stung our faces as we walked up the driveway. Heath and Alison rushed inside to turn on the

Christmas tree lights. From our bay window the blue lights cast a peaceful glow across the snowy yard. I draped my arm around Nita and led her in.

Wrapping paper flew as the children tore into their presents, and Nita and I settled back on the couch to view the happy chaos. Nita had turned the tree into a work of art. The crowning touch was a glorious blond angel perched high at the top. "It looks like Alison," I said.

Alison was so delighted with her big new doll that she granted it the honor of accompanying her to bed. "Told you she'd love it," I reminded Nita as we climbed under the covers. The moaning wind lulled us to sleep.

ROAR! The explosive sound jolted the house. I hadn't been asleep long, and my startled, half-awake mind tried to separate fantasy from reality. The dream again, I thought. But then I sat bolt upright, and suddenly I knew. This was no dream. This time my nightmare was real. The tree really had fallen on our house!

I leapt out of bed and raced across the hall to Alison's room. "Daddy, help!" she was calling frantically. "I'm stuck!"

I couldn't budge the door. It was jammed shut. "Oh, my God," I whispered. "Don't move, honey!" I shouted through the door. "We'll get you out." I grabbed a flashlight and told Nita to call 911. "I'll see if I can get to her from outside."

I was horrified to find the tree filling the front hall, branches whipping in the gale. I stumbled through the family room to a side door. Outside I nearly collided with the massive trunk. Propped up on its giant ball of roots, which had been torn from the earth, it looked prehistoric. I crawled underneath as the rough bark tore at my robe and ripped my flesh. The wind sliced through me. Above the din I heard the distant wail of sirens.

Groping my way to Alison's window I aimed the flashlight beam inside and wiped the icy snow from my eyes. All I could see were branches, tattered insulation and hunks of ceiling strewn about the trunk. Somewhere buried beneath the tree was my daughter, crying faintly, "Daddy! Daddy!"

Someone was standing beside me. "Alison! This is Captain McCullough of the fire department," he called. "Your daddy's with me. Can you move at all?"

"I think I can move my arm," came a brave little voice.

"Good. Push your hand up as high as you can."

Tiny fingers wriggled up through the debris. I breathed a tentative sigh of relief. Firemen rushed to set up lights and heat lamps. They fastened a plastic tarp over the rescue area. Captain McCullough turned to me and said quietly, "This isn't going to be easy, Mr. Gullion."

As I huddled with Nita, and neighbors looked after Heath, a terrifying game of pick-up-sticks slowly unfolded. The night air was filled with the roar of chain saws and the reek of fir pitch as rescuers cut away at the tree and cautiously removed branches as they went. A slight shift of any debris could spell disaster.

Bit by bit they chipped away at the wreckage until, after an hour, Alison's head and shoulders emerged. Her right leg appeared to be crushed under the tree. A fallen two-by-six rafter clamped down on her torso. We could see Alison's new doll squeezed between her chest and the rafter. Apparently she'd fallen asleep clutching it.

McCullough shook his head grimly and called a halt to the work. "We can't risk it," he said. "Show me the crawl space." Moments later he played his flashlight on the area under Alison's room. Limbs a half foot in diameter pierced the floor and stabbed the ground beneath. Again McCullough

shook his head. "We can't cut away the floor without disturbing the tree. *And that tree must not shift.*"

The subzero wind had intensified. Hours had passed and now there was the threat of Alison succumbing to hypothermia. Neighbors rushed in warm blankets and hot-water bottles. A paramedic put his wool ski cap on Alison's head. But I could see she was drifting, her big eyes fluttering. Once or twice her head rolled back. If we didn't get her leg out soon, the surgeons might have to amputate it to free her.

Only one chance was left: Lift the tree. A crane was out of the question. In this wind it would be too unstable. But McCullough had called a towing company that used giant air bags to gently right overturned semi-trailers. "It's a gamble," he warned me. "But we've run out of options."

Huge rubber bags were packed under the tree. A compressor roared to life. Slowly the bags filled with air and swelled against the great fir. Despite the blizzard, I could see sweat bead up on McCullough's tensed brow. My hands trembled as Nita buried her head in my chest, afraid to look.

Suddenly I heard myself praying to the God whose very existence, just hours earlier, I'd doubted. You would have thought I'd be ashamed to ask His help now, but something told me I must. "Please, Lord," I begged, "spare her life. I believe You are there."

The shriek of the compressor was deafening. The bags bulged like great billows, but at first nothing gave.

Then there was movement! Inch by agonizing inch, the tree was lifted. A cry rose from the crowd as paramedics rushed to free Alison and whisk her to a waiting ambulance. Nita and I jumped in with her, and we roared off. Alison smiled weakly. "I'll be okay now, Daddy," she whispered, still grasping her new doll.

That overstuffed doll, it turned out, was possibly just enough of a cushion between the fallen two-by-six rafter and Alison's chest to have saved her life.

The doctors confirmed that she would recover. And Alison's leg was only broken, not crushed.

Christmas Day, Heath and I kicked through the rubble of our house. I'd been thinking about that desperate prayer I'd said, thinking about it a lot. In Alison's room I saw that the bulk of the fir had landed near the southeast wall—right where her bed had been before she'd impulsively moved it. On the trunk directly over where Alison lay when the tree came crashing through, I noticed a wide scar from a recently cut branch—one of those I'd felt such urgency to remove after my dream. That branch might have killed her.

Had God been trying to warn me all along about the tree? To protect us? Had I been blind to God's ways?

In the snow outside what used to be our living room I found the angel from our Christmas tree, the one that looked like Alison. Its wing was broken, just as the angel's wing in my dream had been. As I brushed it off and held it up, Heath came running. "Dad, Dad!" He grabbed the angel. "I've seen this before! In a dream! An angel with a broken wing just like this one!"

Dreams. Does God speak to us through them? The Bible says He does, as well as in many other ways. This much I myself can say: Alison is safe and well. And God is, and always has been, watching over my family.

MR. EVANS' BUS

KYM COLEMAN

F inished with my last exam, I left school in Boston and headed for New York City to spend Christmas with my sister in Queens. I'd only recently come to the U.S. from Liberia, and as my bus pulled into Manhattan's Port Authority late that night I wondered how I would safely find my way to Queens. I grabbed my suitcase and stepped off the bus, searching for a sign to tell me where to go next, but there was none. *Dear God, who should I ask for help?*

In the bus next to mine, a driver in uniform sat alone. "Excuse me," I said. "Could you tell me how to get to Queens?"

"Come aboard. I'll take you wherever you need to go," he said. I gave him my sister's address, hoping he knew the area.

"You'll take me all the way?" I asked.

"Why not?" he said cheerfully. "It's Christmas!"

I got on the empty bus. We introduced ourselves and talked about our holiday plans along the way. Mr. Evans took me right to my sister's door and refused to let me pay him. "I told you, it's Christmas," he laughed.

The next morning I called Port Authority. Without mentioning the free ride in case it would get him in trouble, I gave Mr. Evans a glowing recommendation to be passed on to his employer. But when the man on the phone checked to see which bus line he worked for, his name didn't appear on a single personnel list. I'd expected to see angels at Christmastime—I never thought I'd hitch a ride with one!

INCIDENT AT CHURCH STREET STATION

ERIC LENIHAN

My best buddy, Scott Lobozzo, was home on leave from the Army for the holidays, and a couple other friends and I planned a big reunion up in Orlando. We'd been close as brothers since sixth grade, and things weren't the same when he wasn't around.

Scott was a free spirit, always trying to entertain his friends. But I could count on him no matter what. He'd helped me through some tough times. Once in high school, when I was replaced as goalie on the soccer team and benched, Scott badgered me until I asked the coach to try out for another position. I did and got to play again. Another time, I remember being sick over losing a girl, but Scott slapped me on the back. "She didn't deserve you," he said. The absolute sincerity in his voice made me believe him, and I snapped out of my funk.

The four of us drove to Orlando that December night in 1997, and sat talking at an outdoor café in the Church Street Station entertainment complex. Scott had us laughing, as usual, going on about his escapades in the Army. "It's an adventure," he said. "Next time you see me, I'll be a general."

Same old Scott, I thought. Much as I enjoyed his playfulness, it made me worry about him also. That was Scott, too often acting on impulse. I hoped God would come to his rescue if his *joie de vivre* ever got him into trouble.

"Hey, check that out," said Scott, turning from the café table to point at a freight train rumbling south along the nearby railroad tracks. He stood up. "Anybody want to catch that train?" The rest of us glanced at each other and laughed. Another one of his jokes. Before we could say a word, Scott hopped over the picket fence around the restaurant and sprinted toward the train.

"Let's go!" he shouted. Then, running alongside the train, he reached for one of the handrails.

"Scott!" I called after him, afraid he was going to take this daring game too far.

The rail caught Scott's hand, and I watched in horror as the impact slammed him backward. He stumbled and fell to the ground. The train, moving relentlessly into the night, dragged him under the boxcars and rolled onward, leaving Scott lying on the rails.

I raced over and knelt beside him. His face was chalk white. "My legs," he groaned. Scott had lost part of his left leg on the railroad ties, and his right leg was twisted and blood-soaked.

My mind went blank. The accident had happened so fast. I stood up and ran to the restaurant, shouting to our friends, "Get help! Call 911!" Then I raced back to Scott.

A man stood by the tracks. He was wearing a tan trench coat, tan hat and glasses. "I saw what happened," he said. "Your buddy needs a tourniquet." He started removing his belt. "Right!" I said, following his lead, quickly pulling off my own. The man slipped his belt over Scott's left leg, tightening it above the wounds. I knelt beside him and did the same on Scott's right leg.

"You're going to be okay," I said in the same convincing tone he had used to tell me that my old girlfriend didn't deserve me. I wanted him to believe he was going to be okay. I wanted to believe it too.

Within minutes an ambulance and a police car screeched up. Paramedics ran toward us. I wouldn't leave Scott's side until they slid him into the ambulance and roared off. Then I begged a ride to the hospital with the police officers. "I'm his brother," I said. I loved him like one, anyway.

Scott was in surgery for ten hours, and was given over seventy units of blood. His right leg was saved, and a prosthesis would be fitted for the left so he could walk again. If it hadn't been for the tourniquets, the doctors said, Scott would have died on the tracks. "Your quick thinking saved his life."

"Well, it wasn't me," I tried explaining. "There was this guy in a trench coat. . . ."

Apparently no one had seen him except me. That's when I finally understood that I didn't have to worry so much about Scott. Sure, we'd still look out for each other like brothers. But ultimately our Father was the one who'd look out for us both.

CHAPTER FOUR

CONVEYING PEACE

O morning stars, together
Proclaim the holy birth!
And praises sing to God the King,
And peace to men on earth.

P raise to God. Peace to earth. It's the message of the angel chorus that filled the sky the night of Jesus' birth: "Glory to God in the highest, and on earth peace, good will toward men" (Luke 2:14).

Peace may not be evident on the scale of world politics, but it *is* evident in story after story of the Spirit of Christ calming anxious spirits, one at a time. The writers of the stories in this section tell us of specific Christmas seasons when they sensed, saw or heard angels that conveyed peace to them, in times of tension and need, trauma and desperation, sickness and loss, and even in the face of death.

– E.B.

ANGELS OF FORGIVENESS

SUSAN MAY WARREN

I felt as if I had been slapped. I gasped in horror as I stared at the empty storage room and tried to comprehend my mother-in-law's words: "We even made two hundred dollars!" She had sold all my worldly possessions, without my permission. She was trying to be kind, but in doing so, she had plowed a cavernous furrow through the garden of our friendship. I knew it would never bloom again.

Our family had just returned home after serving as missionaries for four years in Russia. We still had not found a place to live, and my mother-in-law wanted to help by clearing out a room for us in her unfinished basement—in the space our forty boxes of lifetime treasures once occupied. Everything from hand-knit sweaters to homemade quilts was gone. All that was left was a forlorn crate of John Denver records and a bag of used mittens.

She handed me the proceeds of the sale, and it felt like tainted money. I had waited four years to unwrap my wedding china, greet my books and knickknacks, and slip back into my fine dresses. In a brutal instant, my home had gone up in flames. It was humbling to realize that I had put so much value on possessions, but I had, and now I was stripped.

Then I discovered that thirty years of heirloom Christmas ornaments had been sold in the sale. Every year since childhood, my mother had given me a special gift at Christmas, a new and unique tree decoration that symbolized my life for that year, as well as her love for me. The box of ornaments I had so carefully packed had been sold for a dollar; my memories, traded for the price of two candy bars.

A ball of anger swelled in my heart. As I curled in my bed, sobbing out my grief, the ball began to roll. Like a snowball, it gained momentum and became an avalanche burying any tendril of love I had left for the mother of my husband.

Christmas loomed close, and everywhere I went I saw beautiful, glittering Christmas trees. My tree was naked, its green arms bare against the white lights. Where was the golden star with my name etched on it, or my tiny porcelain piano? Memories assaulted me until I surrendered to fury and was entombed in cold bitterness. How could she have done this?

Sometime in January I realized I had missed the joy that came with the Advent season. Joy couldn't penetrate my icy heart. I could barely look at my mother-in-law, despite the fact that she begged my forgiveness.

"I didn't know how much this would hurt you," she sobbed. "I was just trying to help."

I turned a frigid heart to her wrenching plea. Frost laced the edges of our conversations, and, although I said the words, "I forgive you," my soul was an iceberg and I knew I had not.

In the past, my mother-in-law had been my greatest supporter, encouraging me, helping me pack, baby-sitting, stuffing thousands of newsletters. She had cried with me, prayed for me and tolerated my living

in her home. I missed her and knew that if I wanted warmth to re-enter my heart, I had to forgive her. But nothing could ease the ache of losing my memories. I avoided her and resolved to live with the pain.

When we moved away in February, I slammed the door on our relationship.

The following December, three days before Christmas, a parcel with my name on it arrived at our front door. Mystified, I opened it. Then, surrounded by the music of my family's astonished gasps, I unwrapped, one by one, a collection of angel ornaments. From bears with wings and halos to gilded crystal angels holding trumpets, I hung a choir of heavenly hosts on my tree. Finally, I sank into the sofa as my children examined the decorations, *ooh*ing and *aah*ing.

"Who's it from?" my husband asked. I retrieved the box, dug through the tissue, and unearthed a small card. *Merry Christmas—Love, Mom* was scrawled out in my mother-in-law's script. Tears burned my eyes, and as I let them free, my icy tomb of anger began to melt. My mother-in-law was not able to retrieve the past she had so carelessly discarded, but she was hoping to build a future, our future. And it would start with these angels, proclaiming the love and forgiveness that entered our world.

Easter arrived, and with it spring finally flowered in my heart. We descended upon the in-laws for a visit, and I wrapped my husband's mother in a teary embrace. I had lost the little stuffed bunnies my grandmother had knit for me, but I had gained something precious—the abundant fragrance of forgiveness permeating my relationship with my mother-in-law, and the everlasting hope that love can warm the coldest heart.

SLEEP IN HEAVENLY PEACE

LOIS LONNQUIST

I stood at our picture window on a January night. A strong west wind was bending the branches of our birch tree, sending swirls of snow across the lawn. I touched my fingertips to the icy glass, closed the drapes, then sat down on the couch, wrapping myself in my new Christmas robe.

I had gone to bed earlier, but after tossing and turning for an hour I had finally given up and come into the living room to think things out. That afternoon at the office we'd been told that several employees would be laid off. Those of us affected would be notified at week's end. I fretted over the pile of bills that had accumulated and wondered how we would manage if I lost my job. "Don't worry," my husband Del had insisted. But I couldn't help it. As I hugged a sofa pillow and prayed, *Lord, help me trust in Your care*, I recalled a treasured memory of forty years earlier.

It was our first January together. We were so young, nineteen and twenty years old. Married for only ten months, our first baby coming in April, we had dreams and plans, but none were working out.

Del had a job washing windows, but the starting salary was barely enough for us to live on. My difficult pregnancy prevented me from

working. Our home was a small trailer parked in a mobile home court on the outskirts of Spokane, Washington. Sparsely furnished with a drop-leaf table, a folding chair, the backseat from a car and a small bed, the trailer had belonged to a hunter and bore the scars of many trips. It lacked a bathroom, so we had to use the shower and rest rooms in a laundry house nearby.

Nevertheless, we had managed to have a happy Christmas. We bought a little tree and trimmed it with handmade decorations and popcorn. On Christmas Eve we went to our church for the candlelight services, savoring the scent of freshly cut evergreens as we sang carols. Back home we sat on the car-seat couch, drinking hot chocolate to stay warm while we picked names for our baby.

January arrived with bitter cold and snow. Del would go off to work shivering in a light jacket and worn boots, while doctor's orders confined me to bed. Then one freezing morning shortly after Del left for work, the flame in our temperamental fuel-oil heater went out. The winds rattled our flimsy home, blowing through every crack. I put on a coat, wrapped myself in two blankets and counted the hours until Del came home.

By the time he did I was half frozen. Immediately he began working on the old heater. The cold and our frustration set off an exchange of angry words until, at last, the only sound was Del tapping and adjusting the heater.

At 10:00 P.M. he finally got it going again.

For a late supper we ate boiled cabbage and stale bread. Without feeling very thankful, we bowed our heads and said grace. Tears slipped down my cheeks as I picked up my fork, forcing myself to eat. Del sat across from me, looking thin and tired. We barely said a word to each other. I knew he was worried about me and our baby. I wanted to reach out to him, to tell him everything would be okay, but I was so filled with self-pity I couldn't.

Just then we heard footsteps on the wooden crate that served as our doorstep. Who would be coming to see us at this hour?

We waited for the knock. Instead, we heard a child singing, "Silent night, holy night, all is calm, all is bright." The clear, sweet, pure notes came from just outside the door. It was so startling, so comforting, neither of us moved. "Round yon virgin mother and child. Holy infant so tender and mild." The cold, our meager dinner, the ramshackle trailer, none of it mattered. We listened to the angelic tones that floated through the night air. "Sleep in heavenly peace."

Then there was silence. Del and I jumped up at the same time, with the same thought: Why was a child out so late in the cold?

Del opened the door carefully so as not to scare whoever it was. Light spilled onto the wooden step. Fresh snow covered it, and the same untouched white blanket buried the path to our door. Where was the child?

Without even grabbing our coats, we raced outside and walked around our trailer and the homes nearby. Most of them were dark; everyone was inside, asleep. Driven indoors by the cold, we returned and stood in the middle of the trailer amazed.

We had both heard the unmistakable sound of feet on our wooden step and a child's voice lifted in song. Life was hard at the moment, but we knew we would be okay. Del opened his arms and held me close. "We've got each other," he said, "and someone is watching over us."

A few days later Del's supervisor gave him a raise and offered him

overtime hours until spring. The additional income allowed us to move to a small house, and when the baby arrived we managed our medical bills just fine.

Now, four decades later, I began to take stock. We had a beautiful family and a fine home—God had given us so much to be thankful for. We would make it through this crisis, even if I lost my job. All I needed was to have faith.

I went back to the window, opened the drapes and looked at the sky. The clouds were drifting apart, letting the stars shine through, and in my mind I could hear the pure voice of a child singing on the doorstep about heavenly peace, just waiting for me to let it in.

FOUR MYSTERIOUS VISITORS

DAVID WAITE

Last Christmas got off to a promising start. Alison and I and the children—two of our four were still at home—had picked out a tree and its lights were twinkling merrily in the living room. I had lit a fire to take the edge off our raw English air. And then twelve-year-old Matthew hesitantly asked me a question that would have been perfectly natural in any other household: "Dad, would it be all right if I put on some Christmas music?"

Of course," I said, too quickly.

I braced myself. As strains of "Hark! The Herald Angels Sing" began to fill the house, a familiar gnawing sensation grew in the pit of my stomach. *Not again*, I thought. Christmas carols were one of the triggers that could inexplicably bring on a severe anxiety attack. I slipped out of the living room and met Ali in the hallway.

"Are you all right?" she asked. I shrugged. "Do you want to turn off the music?"

"I can't do that," I said. I went upstairs to my office. Work would keep my mind occupied. I tried to focus on a newspaper feature but succeeded only in staring at the impatiently blinking cursor.

I had hoped the old fears would not plague me this Christmas. All my life I had been beset with vague apprehensions and the awful depressions that followed.

The roots weren't hard to find. Born prematurely, forty-nine years ago in the village of Styal near Manchester, England, I spent the first three months of life fighting to survive. I had been born with a shortened and twisted right leg that, later, made walking difficult. In my first week at school a girl pointed at me. "You're a cripple!" she said. She hobbled off in a perfect imitation of my limp that set the other kids laughing.

Being lame of body was not half as bad, though, as being crippled in spirit. My mental woes may have been inherited. My granddad suffered from free-floating fears and so did my father. Dad was so tense that he and Mum were in constant rows, yelling at each other, slamming doors, hurling crockery, then continuing the battle with silence that could last for weeks.

My first serious depression occurred in my early teens. Dad was the village bobby and on his salary we couldn't afford psychiatric help, even if he had believed in it. Antidepressant drugs were in use by 1960, but I was wary of trying these early experimental medicines.

There were glimmers of hope. I became a Christian at eighteen, and for a while I believed this commitment might help me get better. It didn't—not for more than thirty years. Of course I prayed about my anxieties, always in private because I was far too shy to bring up my need at church.

When I married Alison I hoped I was beginning a new, healthier chapter. But along with the joy of a wife and growing family came responsibilities that made the problem worse. Six weeks was the longest I could go without suffering an acute anxiety attack. Little things set the explosions off. A bill coming due. A Christmas carol. The family was ready to leave for church one summer day when I realized my cuff links were missing. It didn't matter because I was wearing a short-sleeved shirt, but I held us up until the cuff links were found.

I was spoiling things for everyone. The best I could do was keep out of the way while depressed. Soon I was spending days on end in my room, as my family waited for me to come around again.

Then on the fifteenth of December last year, a few days after the renewed battle with Christmas carols, I was putting my good foot, the left one, on a step when I stumbled. Searing pain shot through my leg. Within an hour I could not use the leg at all. It was just the kind of incident that usually sank me into a depressive state. Ali offered to pray not only for the leg pain but also for the funk that would almost certainly follow.

What good would prayer do? We had asked God to help us so often. But this time He was about to answer, and in a fashion I could never have anticipated.

Ali prayed for me and my leg did get better, but not the signs of oncoming depression. That evening, just ten days before Christmas, as we were getting ready for bed, Ali remembered that because of the cold weather she had not opened the windows as she usually did to freshen the room. She picked up what she thought was an air-purifying spray and sent a mist all over the room. But the spray turned out to be a sore-muscle balm with a dreadful menthol smell that I've always hated.

"Whew!" I said. "I'll have to sleep in Daniel's room if I want to get any rest." Our oldest son Daniel was in London and his room was empty.

I kissed Ali good night, walked to Daniel's room and turned down the spread on his narrow bed, which was right up against the wall. I climbed

in, turned out the light and lay there staring into the darkness. I was unusually warm and comfortable but still fretting about all sorts of things . . . bills, a close friend in hospital, an assignment that was due.

At first, in the way you can sometimes sense a person looking at you, it seemed to me someone was in the room, focusing attention on me. I thought Alison had stepped in. "Ali?" I whispered.

There was no answer, not a rustling of clothes, not a stirring of air, and yet I knew beyond doubt I was not alone. A friendly presence was near me, at the head of the bed. Had Daniel come home unexpectedly? I whispered his name. Nothing. Maybe it was one of the younger children. "Matthew? Caroline?" No answer.

Slowly I became aware of a second unseen being in the room, this one at the foot of the bed. It seemed to me the two creatures were facing each other. And then I knew there was a third presence too, and a fourth one, these last two facing each other on the left side of the bed . . . impossible since there was no space between the bed and the wall.

I wanted to call Ali, but there was something so benevolent, so full of promise about the four lively presences that I didn't want to do anything that might risk driving them away. I lay perfectly still, strangely warm and expectant.

And then—how did I know this, since I could not see them?—the four creatures began to move toward one another, two on each side of the bed. Their progress was slow and deliberate. They passed one another, turned and repeated the traverse three, four, maybe five times. Every time their paths crossed I felt as if I would burst with joy.

Then abruptly the room was empty. I knew it as surely as I had known a few minutes earlier that angelic creatures were there. The room

was back to normal and I was alone again, yet still filled with ineffable joy. Should I go tell Alison? But tell her what? That I had been visited by four beings I couldn't see? Still debating, I fell into a deep sleep, the best I had had in years.

By the time I surfaced, the children had already left for school. "You'll never believe what happened last night," I said to Ali. I told her as best I could about the mysterious visitors God had sent me. Alison did believe it and was delighted at my newfound joy and peace, though perhaps wondering, as I was, if this calm would last for more than a few days.

Our doubts were misplaced. I enjoyed every minute of the Christmas season. December was followed by a long gray January and February, two months that in the past had been times of distress but were filled with an exultation new to me. The joy even survived a devastating bout I had with the flu. Winter gave way to a spring, a summer and then an autumn of freedom.

Though I can't be sure how long this freedom will last, I am beginning to believe the victory is permanent. It's not that I've shed pressures like bills and problems at work. But today I confront these issues with a positive attitude unlike my past fearfulness.

Christmas is once again just around the corner. Thanks to my heavenly visitors, I'm anticipating another joy-filled season and I am going to make a statement to that effect. This year I have bought a present for the entire family, a small but very special gift I hope we will use a lot . . . a CD of the world's best-loved Christmas carols.

RESCUED

RONALD HUGHES

One brochure was all it took for my wife Judy and me to fall in love with Hawaii. Maui at Christmastime! We were there with our two kids on our dream vacation.

Waves crashed right outside our hotel room. The ocean called to me on the balcony. The sky was cloudless, a brilliant blue. This really was paradise. "Don't even unpack," I said to the family. "Let's hit the beach before the sun goes down." Judy grabbed some towels, and we were off.

I led the way to an ancient lava rock wall that had formed on the beach. "Follow me," I said, and found a way to get up top. The clear blue water stretched on endlessly. We walked the length of the wall, which jutted out into the ocean for about fifty feet before coming to a point. There it hooked back into a tiny cove.

"Look at those beautiful fish," Judy said. Red, yellow, blue—every color of the rainbow flashed in the sun just below the surface.

"Why don't we get some snorkel gear tomorrow?" I said to Judy. "We can explore underwater and maybe get a good look at those fish up close."

The next day Judy and I rented snorkels and diving masks from the hotel. We made our way down the crowded beach. The kids got right to work playing in the sand at the water's edge. "Your mother and I are going for a swim," I told them. "We'll all go in the water when we get back."

Judy and I plunged into the ocean. The water was crystal clear; I could see all the way to the bottom, about thirty or forty feet down. I swam alongside the rocks till I got to where the wall hooked. I continued on around the point and turned to look for Judy. She wasn't behind me. What happened? I wondered. Waves started to kick up a bit. I eased back to the point, my head above water.

I heard a shout: "Help! Ronnie!"

I only had to take a few strokes before I saw my wife. She'd swum past the point. She sputtered and coughed, barely treading water. She was in trouble.

Water must have gotten down her snorkel. "Judy!" I called. "Hang on!"

I had my Red Cross lifesaving certificate. I knew what could happen. Judy was a strong swimmer, but she was panicking. If I swam out to her—if I could reach her—I had to grab her just the right way. Otherwise she might latch onto me and take me under with her. I thought about our children. What would they do with both of us gone? But my wife needed me now.

Frantic, I looked around for other people. A sailboat was anchored about twenty yards from the beach. Two guys stood on the deck talking. "Help!" I shouted. "Help!" I clung to the rocks with one hand and waved my free arm wildly over my head, shouting as loud as I possibly could. They were so close I could recognize the brand of soda one of them held.

But the two paid me no mind. *Can they hear me?* I looked back at

Judy. The waves had pulled her even farther away. "Judy! Judy, can you hear me?" I shouted. "Try not to panic."

Something moved beneath me. I stuck my face mask into the water. A group of scuba divers scuttled along the bottom in single file.

I slapped the water to try to get their attention. It wasn't any use. They kept on going. Again I saw movement in the water below. Once more I stuck my head under. A very large bald man clung to the lava wall maybe eight feet down. He was alone. Was he studying the sea life growing on the rocks? I slapped the water again.

The man turned his head to look up at me. I waved, motioning for him to come up. *Please, help us. Please.*

He floated up until he broke the surface of the water right next to me. He was about six foot five. He wore goggles like the ones I'd seen on Japanese pearl divers, but his size made the goggles seem oddly small.

"Help me!" I begged. "My wife!"

He looked Judy's way. She was still coughing, trying desperately to stay afloat. "You're going to be okay," he said calmly to Judy. "Come to me."

He spoke in a regular tone of voice. I couldn't imagine how Judy could have heard him. Yet I knew she had because the panic in her face disappeared. I saw that she was back in control.

Judy broke into an overhand stroke and swam toward me, crashing her way right through the swells.

The man turned back to the wall and sank, as if to go back about his business. Didn't he want to wait to be sure we were all right?

Judy reached me, and I hugged her tight. "The waves were pulling me out," she said, shaking. "I was so scared I couldn't think to swim."

I was shaking too. I didn't know what to say for myself. The thought that I'd failed my wife miserably kept going through my head. If I'd just had the wherewithal of the bald man in the goggles, if only I'd spoken to Judy the way he had, I could have saved her.

Once we'd calmed down I helped Judy to shore. The kids were still filling buckets with sand and making castles. They had no idea of the danger we'd been in. And we didn't dare tell them.

We never told anyone what happened. We tried talking about that day to each other, but every time we started we both got choked up. Our emotions wouldn't let us relive those terrible moments of Christmas vacation.

Until one Saturday morning years later. Our pastor dropped by the house unannounced. Judy and I sat with him in the living room. I never knew just what he was going to say, and that day was no different. "Have you ever had an encounter with an angel?" he asked, right out of the blue.

"Maybe," I told him. That's when it came to me, a picture in my mind of the bald man with the pearl-diver goggles. There had been something more than a little unusual about him. . . .

I started telling the story of that fateful Christmas Day. And for the first time ever, I didn't get choked up. My voice remained calm. My tone was as regular as the bald man's voice had sounded when he called out to Judy. "Come to me" was all it had taken. "And then he disappeared underwater," I finished. "Just like that."

"No," Judy said. "That's not the way it happened at all."

I looked at her. What had I left out?

"There was a man by me," she said. "He came up from the deep water below. He had dark hair and a beard, and he didn't say a word. He grabbed my arm so tight it hurt. And then he carried me over to you, Ronnie."

But that is not what I saw, I thought. *There was only one man. The bald one, by me.*

"There was no one with you," Judy insisted. "I didn't take my eyes off you the whole time."

But, then, how could that be? I don't know. The only way I can explain it is that we both got an angel of our own. One came to me, calming my fears. And one held on to Judy, bringing her back to me.

It was a dream vacation, all right, but what happened to us was no dream. It was real. And it was a Christmas we will never forget. Never.

A STRANGER OF LIGHT
IN THE CANCER WARD

KELSEY TYLER

The bad news came January 6, 1981.

Until then, Melissa and Chris Deal were by most standards one of the happiest couples anywhere. They were in their early twenties, lived in Nashville, Tennessee, and shared a passion for country music and the outdoors. They were constantly finding new ways to enjoy each other's company, whether by mountain-biking, hiking or playing tennis together. Attractive and athletic, Melissa and Chris seemed to live a charmed life in which everything went their way.

That was before Chris got sick. At first the couple believed he was only suffering from a severe cold. Then they wondered if perhaps he had contracted mononucleosis. But the doctors chose to run blood tests; and finally, on that cold January day, Chris's condition was diagnosed as acute lymphatic leukemia. At age twenty-eight, Chris was suffering with the deadliest form of childhood cancer.

During the next three months, Chris's cancer slipped into remission and he stayed the picture of health. Muscular at six feet two inches and two hundred pounds, Chris looked more like a professional athlete than a

man suffering from leukemia. During that time, Chris continued to work and neither he nor Melissa spent much time talking about his illness.

At the end of that period, doctors discovered that Chris's brother was a perfect match for a bone marrow transplant. But before the operation could be scheduled, Chris's remission ended dramatically and he became very ill.

"I'm afraid he's too weak to undergo a transplant," Chris's doctor explained as the couple sat in his office one afternoon. "The cancer has become very aggressive."

The doctor recommended that Chris be admitted to Houston's cancer hospital, M. D. Anderson, for continuous treatment in hopes of forcing the disease into remission. Within a week, Chris and Melissa had taken medical leaves of absence from their jobs and both moved into the Houston hospital. The nurses generously set up a cot for Melissa so that she could stay beside Chris, encouraging him and furnishing him strength during his intensive chemotherapy and radiation treatments.

Living in a cancer ward was very depressing for the Deals, who had previously seen very little of death and dying. The couple talked often about how their lives had become little more than a nightmare in which Chris fought for his life amidst other people like him, people with no real chance of overcoming their cancer. Chris began to spend a great deal of time in prayer, asking God to take care of Melissa no matter what happened to him. He prayed for remission, but also asked God for the strength to accept his death if his time had come to die.

Months passed and doctors began to doubt whether Chris's cancer would ever be in remission again. By Christmas . . . Chris weighed only one hundred pounds. His eyes were sunken into his skull, and he had lost nearly all of his strength. He was no longer able to walk and only rarely found the energy needed to sit up in bed. Doctors told Melissa that there was nothing more they could do.

"I don't think he has much longer, Melissa," one doctor said. "I want you to be ready."

On January 4, Melissa fell into a deeper sleep than usual and was awakened at three in the morning by a nurse.

"Mrs. Deal," the nurse said, her voice urgent, "wake up! Your husband has gone."

Thinking that her husband had died in his sleep, Melissa sat straight up, afraid of what she might see. But Chris's hospital bed was empty.

"He's gone! Where is he, what happened? Where did you take him?" she asked frantically.

"We haven't moved him, ma'am," the nurse said quickly. "He must have gotten up and walked somewhere. We came in to check his vital signs and he was gone."

Melissa shook her head, willing herself to think clearly. "He can't walk. You know that." She was frustrated and her voice rose a level.

Even if her husband had found the strength to get out of bed and shuffle into the hallway, he would have been seen. Chris's room was on the circular eleventh floor of the cancer hospital, and the nurses' station was a round island in the center of the floor. There was no way Chris could have gotten up and walked out of his room without someone spotting him. Especially since each of his arms was attached to intravenous tubing.

The nurse appeared flustered and shaken, and suddenly Melissa jumped to her feet and ran from the room. As she ran toward the elevators, Melissa's

eyes caught a slight movement in the eleventh-floor chapel. Heading for the door and peering inside, Melissa was stunned by what she saw.

Inside the chapel, with his back to the door, Chris was sitting casually in one of the pews and talking with a man. He was unfettered by intravenous tubing, and although still very thin, he appeared to be almost healthy.

Melissa was filled with anger. Why had Chris left without saying anything? And who was this man? Melissa knew she had never seen him before, and he wasn't dressed like a doctor. Where had he come from at three in the morning? Melissa stared through the window trying to make sense of what was happening.

After several minutes passed, Melissa walked into the chapel toward her husband. At the same time, the stranger looked down at the floor, almost as if he did not want Melissa to see his face. She noted that he was dressed in a red-checked flannel work shirt, blue jeans and a brand-new pair of lace-up work boots. His white hair was cut short to his head, and his skin was so white it appeared transparent. Melissa turned toward Chris, still keeping one eye on the man across from him.

"Chris?" she said, questioningly. "Are you all right? Where have you been?"

"Melissa, it's okay," Chris said, laughing casually and appearing stronger than he had in months. "I'll be back in the room in a little while."

At that instant, she turned toward the stranger and he looked up at her. Melissa was struck by the brilliance of his clear blue eyes. *Who was he?* she wondered. How was he able to make Chris laugh and appear so at ease when only hours earlier he had been barely able to move? Melissa stared at the man, mesmerized by the look in his eyes and searching for an explanation as to his existence.

"What's going on?" she asked, turning back toward her husband.

"Melissa, please, I'll be back in the room soon!" Chris's voice was gentle but adamant. Melissa knew that he wanted her to leave them alone.

Reluctantly, Melissa turned to go, making her way back to the center station where she informed Chris's nurses that he was in the chapel. They were relieved and did not attempt to bring him back to his room.

For thirty minutes, Melissa waited alone in the hospital room until finally Chris joined her. Melissa almost didn't recognize him. With a wide grin on his face and a twinkle in his eyes, Chris appeared to be full of energy as he walked toward her with a strength he hadn't had before. He was obviously happy and at peace with himself.

"Okay, I want to know who that man was. Why were you talking to him? What did he say? And how come you're walking so well? What happened?" Melissa fired the questions at her husband in succession and he began laughing.

"Melissa, he was an angel."

His happiness and the way Chris spoke those words left no doubt in Melissa's mind that he believed what he had said was the truth. She was silent a moment, allowing herself to ponder the possibility that the man had indeed been an angel.

"I believe you," she said softly, reaching toward her husband and taking his hand in hers. "Tell me about it."

Chris told her that he had been jerked awake and instantly experienced an overpowering urge to go to the chapel. His tubing had already been removed, something none of the nurses remembered doing when they were asked later. As he moved to climb out of bed and begin walking, he was suddenly able to do so without any of his usual weakness.

When he got to the chapel, he quietly moved into a pew and kneeled to pray. He was praying silently when he heard a voice.

"Are you Chris Deal?" the voice asked gently.

"Yes," Chris answered, curiously unafraid of the voice.

At that instant, he turned around and the man was there, dressed in a flannel shirt and jeans. The man sat directly across from Chris, their knees almost touching. For a moment the man said nothing. When he spoke, Chris had the feeling he already knew the man.

"Do you need forgiveness for anything?" the man asked.

Chris hung his head, his eyes welling up with tears. For years he had held bitter and resentful feelings toward a relative he'd known most of his life. He had always known it was wrong to harbor such hatred, but he had never asked for forgiveness. Slowly, Chris looked up and nodded, explaining the situation to the man.

The man told Chris that God had forgiven him. "What else is bothering you?"

"Melissa. My wife," Chris said, the concern showing on his face. "I'm worried about her. What's going to happen to her?"

The man smiled peacefully. "She will be fine."

The man knelt alongside Chris, and for the next twenty minutes the two men prayed together. Finally, the man turned toward Chris and smiled.

"Your prayers have been answered, Chris. You can go now."

Chris thanked the man, and although nothing had been said he somehow was certain the man was an angel.

"And then I came back here," Chris said cheerfully.

Suddenly Melissa leapt to her feet. "I have to find him," she said as she left the room. . . .

Melissa returned to Chris's hospital room where he was sitting, his arms crossed in front of him, with a knowing look on his face.

"Didn't find him, right?" Chris said, grinning.

"Where did he go? I really want to talk to him." Melissa was frustrated, baffled by the man's sudden disappearance.

"I guess he went to wherever he came from, honey. He did what he came to do and he left."

The next day when Chris awoke, even more energetic than he had been the night before, both Melissa and Chris thought he was miraculously in remission. He was happy and content and spent much of the day visiting the other patients on the floor and offering them encouragement by praying with them or merely listening to them. Many physical manifestations of his illness seemed to have lessened or disappeared as mysteriously as the man who had visited them.

Then, two days later, Melissa awoke to find Chris staring at her strangely.

Suddenly nervous, Melissa sat up in bed. "What?" she asked.

"I dreamed about Bill last night," Chris said, clearly confused by the dream. "You told me to tell you if I ever dreamed about Bill."

Bill, Chris's best friend, had died in a car accident the year before. For reasons that were unclear to her, Melissa believed that if Chris ever dreamed about Bill, it meant Chris's death was imminent. She hadn't told Chris these thoughts but had asked him to tell her if he ever dreamed about Bill.

Now Melissa was confused. Chris couldn't be near death. He looked vibrant and strong. And if his prayers had been answered, as the flannel-shirted man had told him, then he must have been on his way to recovery. Something wasn't making sense.

"What about the angel?" she asked Chris, her voice filled with anxiety.

Chris shrugged. "I don't know. You just asked me to tell you if I ever dreamed about Bill." Something in Chris's face told Melissa he knew why she had considered the dream significant.

That afternoon, Chris suffered a pulmonary hemorrhage. He began bleeding from his mouth and nose, and immediately there were dozens of doctors and medical experts swarming around, desperately trying to save his life. Melissa moved to a place behind Chris's head and placed her hands on his shoulders.

"Come on, Chris," she shouted frantically. "Stay with me!" At that moment one of the doctors asked her to step aside so they could work on him.

Melissa backed up slowly and found a spot in the room against the wall where she sank down to the floor and buried her head in her hands.

While the doctors hurried about Chris, shouting "Code blue!" and trying to save his life, she began to pray. Almost instantly, she felt a peace wash over her and realized that this was part of God's plan. Chris had prayed that she would be all right, and at that instant she knew she would be, no matter what happened.

That afternoon, minutes before he was pronounced dead, exactly one year after being diagnosed with cancer, Chris called out Melissa's name.

"It's okay, honey," she whispered, her tear-covered face gazing upward. "It's okay."

Now, more than ten years later, Melissa believes that Chris's prayers had indeed been answered that night when he was visited by the man she believes was an angel. Since his time on earth was running short, he had been given the gift of peace, of accepting his fate and not fighting it in fear. Also, he had been released from the bondage of bitterness and hatred and graced with the gift of God's forgiveness. That fact was evident in the happiness and contentment of his final days. And finally, Melissa had survived Chris's death and came out stronger for the ordeal—another answer to Chris's prayer.

Although there are people who might try to explain or argue about the identity of Chris's visitor that night, Melissa saw him, looked him in the eyes and watched the transformation his visit made in Chris's life. As far as she's concerned, there will never be any explanation other than the one Chris gave her that same night: "Melissa, he was an angel."

AN ANGEL'S
SHALOM SHADOW

PAMELA ROSEWELL

*In 1976 Pam Rosewell took a job as a younger companion
to Corrie ten Boom, who soon moved to California from Holland,
retiring at age eighty-six from her worldwide ministry of
reconciliation after the Second World War. In 1978 Corrie
had the first of three strokes that left her bedridden and
virtually speechless. Along with other round-the-clock caretakers,
including those mentioned in this story,
Pam continued to serve Corrie until her death in 1983.*

At Christmas, a year after the third severe stroke, Tante Corrie was feeling very unwell, and although there was much peace in Shalom House, the whole team was tired. Outside in the world around us people were busily preparing for the season. There were colored lights on many of the houses, and the atmosphere was full of activity, very different to the scene inside Tante Corrie's bedroom.

Ruth, whose evening knock was always welcome, said to me a couple of days before Christmas Eve, "You know that verse in Hebrews,

'Are not all angels ministering spirits sent to serve those who will inherit salvation?'"

"Yes," I said, wondering what was coming next.

"Well, I think that Tante Corrie has angels in her bedroom."

"What do you mean?"

It seemed that every evening recently, Ruth had witnessed a shadow cast on the bed as if somebody had passed along beside the night light at the foot of the bed. But no one else was there. And there was a strong sense of comfort and peace in the room at the same time. "I think it's an angel," she concluded.

"Really," I said. "That is very interesting," not adding what I was really thinking: Ruth was seeing things. Yet Ruth was a practical woman, having grown up on a farm, and she saw things very simply. In that way she reminded me of Tante Corrie. It was not like her to be imagining angels. *She must be very tired*, I concluded.

The next day, however, Lotte mentioned that she, too, had seen a shadow in Tante Corrie's room. There was something wrong with the bulb of the night light, I decided, and exchanged it for a new one.

"Have you seen any shadows in Tante Corrie's room?" I asked Bernice when she appeared for weekend duty a couple of nights later.

"As a matter of fact I have," she replied. "At first I thought it was head-lights from cars on the street. But that can't be it, because there have always been cars outside and their lights have not caused this kind of shadow."

The next day it was again my turn at Tante Corrie's bedside. In the near dark, I wondered if I would see an angel. Surely they could not all have imagined it. For quite a while I saw nothing unusual.

But when I had stopped looking and was sitting quietly next to Tante

Corrie, I saw what the others had seen. There was a shadow in the room—not a dark hovering thing, but, if it is possible, a bright shadow. And at once I was overcome by a sense of comfort and peace, like the times when you do not realize you have been tense, but, upon heaving a sigh of relaxation, realize you were. *Shalom.* Peace.

When we talked about it later, we agreed that God was reminding us that we were not alone as we accompanied Tante Corrie—as far as we were permitted—through a very long valley of the shadow of death.

CHAPTER FIVE

BLESSING WITH GIFTS

How silently, how silently,
The wondrous gift is given!
So God imparts to human hearts
The blessings of his heaven.

I n II Corinthians 9:15, the apostle Paul exclaims, "Thanks be to God, for his indescribable gift!"—his Son, born as a babe in Bethlehem. Because that wondrous gift is at the heart of our Christmas celebration, we find joy in giving as well as receiving holiday gifts.

The stories in this section are written by men and women who played a role in giving gifts to others. But in each case there seems more to the story than mere family-centered or neighborly generosity. God is at work behind the scenes, orchestrating events, whispering messages, dispatching angels to impart "the blessings of his heaven." Eileen Fick's "In a Jam" is a short, fun reminder of God's gift-giving help. The longer stories, by Elizabeth English, Chad Hinkson, Marguerite Nixon, and Wayne Montgomery, show the writers as unwittingly meeting human spiritual and physical needs.

— E.B.

"GO TO THE STORE"

ELIZABETH ENGLISH

Herman and I finally locked our store and dragged ourselves home to South Caldwell Street. It was 11:00 P.M., Christmas Eve, 1949. We were dog tired.

Ours was one of those big old general appliance stores that sold everything from refrigerators and toasters and record players to bicycles and dollhouses and games. We'd sold almost all of our toys; and all of the layaways, except one package, had been picked up.

Usually Herman and I kept the store open until everything had been picked up. We knew we wouldn't have waked up very happy on Christmas morning knowing that some little child's gift was back on the layaway shelf. But the person who had put a dollar down on that package never appeared.

Early Christmas morning, our twelve-year-old son Tom, Herman and I were out under the tree opening up gifts. But, I'll tell you, there was something very humdrum about this Christmas. Tom was growing up; he hadn't wanted any toys—just clothes and games. I missed his childish exuberance of past years.

As soon as breakfast was over, Tom left to visit his friend next door.

And Herman disappeared into the bedroom, mumbling, "I'm going back to sleep. There's nothing left to stay up for anyway."

So there I was alone, doing the dishes and feeling very let down. It was nearly 9:00 A.M., and sleet mixed with snow cut the air outside. The wind rattled our windows, and I felt grateful for the warmth of the apartment. *Sure glad I don't have to go out on a day like today*, I thought to myself, picking up the wrappings and ribbons strewn around the living room.

And then it began. Something I'd never experienced before. A strange, persistent urge. "Go to the store," it seemed to say.

I looked at the icy sidewalk outside. *That's crazy*, I said to myself. I tried dismissing the thought, but it wouldn't leave me alone. *Go to the store.*

Well, I wasn't going to go. I'd never gone to the store on Christmas Day in all the ten years we'd owned it. No one opened shop on that day. There wasn't any reason to go, I didn't want to, and I wasn't going to.

For an hour I fought that strange feeling. Finally, I couldn't stand it any longer, and I got dressed.

"Herman," I said, feeling silly, "I think I'll walk down to the store."

Herman woke up with a start. "Whatever for? What are you going to do there?"

"Oh, I don't know," I replied lamely. "There's not much to do here. I just think I'll wander down."

He argued against it a little, but I told him that I'd be back soon. "Well, go on," he grumped, "but I don't see any reason for it."

I put on my gray wool coat and a gray tam, then my galoshes and my red scarf and gloves. Once outside, none of those garments seemed to help. The wind cut right through me and the sleet stung my cheeks. I groped my way along the mile down to 117 East Park Avenue, slipping and sliding all the way.

I shivered, and I tucked my hands inside the pockets to keep them from freezing. I felt ridiculous. I had no business being out in that bitter chill.

There was the store just ahead. The sign announced Radio-Electronic Sales and Service, and the big glass windows jutted out onto the sidewalk. *But, what in the world?* I wondered. In front of the store stood two little boys, huddled together. One about nine, and the other six.

"Here she comes!" yelled the older one. He had his arm around the younger. "See, I told you she would come," he said jubilantly.

They were little black children, and they were half frozen. The younger one's face was wet with tears, but when he saw me, his eyes opened wide and his sobbing stopped.

"What are you two children doing out here in this freezing rain?" I scolded, hurrying them into the store and turning up the heat. "You should be at home on a day like this!" They were poorly dressed. They had no hats or gloves, and their shoes barely held together. I rubbed their small, icy hands, and got them up close to the heater.

"We've been waiting for you," replied the older. They had been standing outside since 9:00 A.M., the time I normally open the store.

"Why were you waiting for me?" I asked, astonished.

"My little brother Jimmy didn't get any Christmas." He touched Jimmy's shoulder. "We want to buy some skates. That's what he wants. We have these three dollars. See, Miss Lady," he said, pulling the money from his pocket.

I looked at the dollars in his hand. I looked at their expectant faces. And then I looked around the store. "I'm sorry," I said, "but we've sold

almost everything. We have no ska. . ." Then my eye caught sight of the layaway shelf with its one lone package. I tried to remember . . . Could it be. . . ?

"Wait a minute," I told the boys. I walked over, picked up the package, unwrapped it and, miracle of miracles, there was a pair of skates!

Jimmy reached for them. *Lord*, I said silently, *let them be his size.*

And miracle added upon miracle, they were his size.

When the older boy finished tying the laces on Jimmy's right foot and saw that the skate fit—perfectly—he stood up and presented the dollars to me.

"No, I'm not going to take your money," I told him. I couldn't take his money. "I want you to have these skates, and I want to use your money to get some gloves for your hands."

The two boys just blinked at first. Then their eyes became like saucers, and their grins stretched wide when they understood I was giving them the skates, that I didn't want their three dollars.

What I saw in Jimmy's eyes was like a blessing. It was pure joy, and it was beautiful. My low spirits rose.

After the children had warmed up, I turned down the heater, and we walked out together. As I locked the door, I turned to the older brother and said, "How lucky that I happened to come along when I did. If you'd stood there much longer, you'd have frozen. But how did you boys know I would come?"

I wasn't prepared for his reply. His gaze was steady, and he answered me softly. "I knew you would come," he said. "I asked Jesus to send you."

The tingles in my spine weren't from the cold, I knew. God had planned this.

As we waved good-bye, I turned home to a brighter Christmas than I had left. Tom brought his friend over to our house. Herman got out of bed; his father "Papa" English and sister Ella came by. We had a wonderful dinner and a wonderful time.

But the one thing that made that Christmas really wonderful was the one thing that makes every Christmas wonderful—Jesus was there.

IN A JAM

EILEEN FICK

Holding several jars of my homemade nectarine jam, I carefully made my way downstairs to store them in the cellar. It was a particularly good batch and I couldn't wait for my grandson Mark, the pickiest of eaters, to taste it.

"Try this," I said the next morning, giving him a piece of toast topped with a dollop of jam. Mark couldn't get enough of it. In fact, it was a hit with the whole family. Every couple of days I had to get another jar from the cellar.

As Christmas approached, I knew exactly the gift for Mark: his very own jar of nectarine jam. But after looking high and low in our cellar, I couldn't find a single one left. *Have I used the last of it?* Nectarines were out of season, but I checked the grocery stores anyway. I'd have to make another (inferior?) batch. We all looked for nectarines without any luck. Finally I searched the cellar again. I moved dozens of jars and cans around, only to be disappointed. Then, a couple days before Christmas, my husband Jerry was about to head into town. "Remember, if you see . . ." He cut me off. "I know, I know—nectarines," he said. But he returned empty-handed. In desperation, I made yet another trip to the cellar, and went through every item on the shelves. Nothing. I gave up and leaned back against the canned tomatoes. *Lord, I just need one jar, one tiny jar of jam, for Mark.*

I turned to shut off the light and stood in disbelief. There on top of the tomato jars—in plain view—were three small jars of the precious nectarine jam. I ran upstairs to tell Jerry I had found the jam. "Can you believe it?" I marveled. "After three searches . . ."

"Four," he said. "I went to the cellar and looked too."

My daughter heard us talking. "Make that five searches," she said. "I knew how badly you wanted that jam for Mark."

My grandson agreed that those three jars tasted even better than the rest of the batch. I wonder if that was because of some heavenly ingredient sprinkled in by the angel who delivered them.

GUIDED BY THE SPIRIT

CHAD HINKSON

I set about checking the instruments in preparation for my last flight of the day, a short hop from Atlanta to Macon, Georgia. It was 7:30 P.M. Christmas Eve, but instead of forking into Mom's turkey dinner, I was busy getting other people home to their families. Above the low buzz of talking passengers, I heard a rustle behind me. I looked over my shoulder. Just outside the cockpit doorway was a fresh-faced boy of about nine gazing intently at the flight deck. At my glance he started to turn away.

"Hold up," I called. "Come on in here." I had been about his age when I first saw a flight panel lit up like a Christmas tree—I could hardly wait to get my pilot's wings. But now that I was twenty-four and first officer at a commuter airline, I wondered if I'd made the right choice. Here I was spending my first Christmas Eve away from home, and what was I accomplishing? How was I making my mark in the world, let alone doing God's work, just hauling people from city to city?

The boy stepped cautiously into the cockpit.

"My name's Chad," I said, sticking out my hand.

With a shy smile he put his hand in mine. "I'm Sam."

He turned to the empty seat beside me. "Is that for the captain?"

"It sure is—that's where Captain Jim sits." I patted the worn fabric. "Would you like to try it out?"

Sam blinked at me from under his ball cap. "I don't know . . . I mean . . . well, sure—if it's okay."

I lowered the seat so he could slide into it. The captain loved to give demonstrations of the plane's gadgets to kids, but what would he think about one sitting in his seat? *Well, it's Christmas,* I thought.

I glanced out at the luggage carts being wheeled toward the plane, thinking of the gifts I wouldn't be able to give in person to my parents and friends the next day. Sam told me he and his family had flown in from Memphis. I checked my watch. The captain would be in any minute, but Sam looked so thrilled, I didn't want to cut short his fun. I gave the instrument panel another once-over, telling Sam what each button and lever did.

Finally Captain Jim clambered aboard. "Howdy, partner." He gave Sam a broad grin. "You know, son," he drawled, "I don't mind you staying with us for a while if you'll switch with me."

Sam let the captain take his place and I made introductions.

We began reviewing the prestart checklist. I kept thinking the captain would send Sam away, but the boy was still peering over my shoulder when the ramp agent radioed to ask if we were ready to turn on the first engine in start sequence, number four.

I relayed the question to the captain, who was studying the weather reports. "I'm still going over these," he said. "You guys go ahead and start it."

"Okay, starting . . ." I said, positioning the switches. Then I did a double take. "Did you say 'you guys'?"

"Yeah, go ahead."

I looked over at the captain, and back at the flight panel. "Right."

I flicked on the plane's flashing red beacon to signal the start. Then I turned to my new assistant. "You ever start an airplane before, Sam?"

Eyes wide, he shook his head. Following my instructions, Sam carefully turned a knob on the overhead console that switched on the igniters. Then he pressed a button as big as his hand to start the engine. Finally, with both hands he slid forward a lever to introduce the fuel. The engine hummed to life.

Sam slowly let go of the lever and stepped back, awestruck. He'd gotten to start an airplane—an honest-to-goodness airliner. I'm not sure if I'd have believed it myself at his age.

I thanked Sam for helping us out.

"No, thank you, sir," Sam said. "This was really great!"

As he backed out of the doorway into the cabin, the plane resonated with the sound of the engine he'd started. "You have a merry Christmas, son, you hear?" the captain said.

Sam looked like he was about to cry with happiness. "I will, sir, I will. Thank you!" With one last look at the flight deck he turned and walked down the aisle. We started up the other engines, took off, and arrived in Macon about forty minutes later.

Early Christmas morning, as we settled into the cockpit for the trip back to Atlanta, one of the gate agents ducked in. "Hey, guys, some kid's mother came by this morning. She wanted to make sure I thanked you for showing her son around last night. Said he couldn't stop talking about the cockpit. She left this for you."

The gate agent set a red tin on the center console.

"Well, I'll be," the captain said. He bit into one of the chocolate chip cookies from the tin. Then he unfolded the note taped to its cover and

read it silently. He sighed deeply and turned to me, "Boy's got cancer," he said, and read the note aloud:

Dear Sirs,

Thank you for allowing Sam to watch you work on Christmas Eve night. Sam has cancer and has been undergoing chemotherapy in Memphis. This is the first time he has been home since the treatment began. We drove Sam up to the hospital, but since he loves airplanes, we decided to fly him back home. I am not sure if he will ever get to fly again. His doctor has said that Sam may have only a few months left.

Sam has always dreamed of becoming an airline pilot. The flight we took from Memphis to Atlanta was exhilarating for him. He wasn't sure flying on one of your "little" airplanes would be as much fun, but you two gentlemen gave him the greatest Christmas gift imaginable. For a few short minutes his dream came true, thanks to you.

I looked out at the runway gleaming before us in the sun. When I turned back to Jim, he was still staring at the note.

A flight attendant came in and said the passengers were ready for departure. She stowed the cookies away and we went through the checklist. Then Captain Jim cleared his throat and called out, "Starting number four."

I'd wanted to be home with my loved ones, exchanging gifts for the holidays. But that little boy showed me that sometimes the most important gifts we give are given unwittingly and the most precious ones we get come from strangers. I can serve God's purpose no matter where I am, as long as I let the spirit that moved me that night guide me always.

UNEXPECTED CHRISTMAS

MARGUERITE NIXON

We were well over halfway to our farm in East Texas when the storm broke. Lightning flashed, thunder crashed, and a tree fell with a great ripping noise. When the rain poured in such a flood that we could not see the road, my husband drove off on to what seemed to be a bit of clearing deep in the piney woods.

As we waited, I sensed we would not get to the farm that night to celebrate Christmas Eve with our family. We were sitting there, miserable and dejected, when I heard a knocking on my window. A man with a lantern stood there beckoning us to follow him. My husband and I splashed after him up the path to his house.

A woman with a lamp in her hand stood in the doorway of an old house; a boy of about twelve and a little girl stood beside her. We went in soaked and dripping, and the family moved aside in order that we might have the warmth of the fire. With the volubility of city people, my husband and I began to talk, explaining our plans. And with the quietness of people who live in the silence of the woods, they listened.

"The bridge on Caney Creek is out. You are welcome to spend the night with us," the man said. And though we told them we thought it was

an imposition, especially on Christmas Eve, they insisted. After we had visited a while longer, the man got up and took the Bible from the mantel. "It's our custom to read the story from St. Luke on Christmas Eve," he said, and without another word he began:

"And she brought forth her firstborn Son, and wrapped him in swaddling clothes, and laid him in a manger. . . ."

The children sat up eagerly, their eyes bright in anticipation, while their father read on: "And there were in the same country shepherds abiding in the field, keeping watch over their flocks by night." I looked at his strong face. He could have been one of them.

When he finished reading and closed the Bible, the little children knelt by their chairs. The mother and father were kneeling, and without any conscious will of my own I found myself joining them. Then I saw my husband, without any embarrassment at all, kneel also.

When we arose, I looked around the room. There were no brightly wrapped packages or cards, only a small, unadorned holly tree on the mantel. Yet the spirit of Christmas was never more real to me.

The little boy broke the silence. "We always feed the cattle at twelve o'clock on Christmas Eve. Come with us."

The barn was warm and fragrant with the smell of hay and dried corn. A cow and a horse greeted us, and there was a goat with a tiny, woolly kid that came up to be petted. *This is like the stable where the Baby was born*, I thought. *Here is the manger, and the gentle animals keeping watch.*

When we returned to the house, there was an air of festivity and the serving of juice and fruitcake. Later, we bedded down on a mattress made of corn shucks. As I turned into a comfortable position, they rustled

under me and sent up a faint fragrance exactly like that in the barn. My heart said, "You are sleeping in the stable like the Christ Child did."

As I drifted into a profound sleep, I knew that the light coming through the old pine shutters was the Star shining on that quiet house.

The family all walked down the path to the car with us the next morning. I was so filled with the Spirit of Christmas they had given me that I could find no words. Suddenly I thought of the gifts in the back seat of our car for our family.

I began to hand them out. My husband's gray woolen socks went to the man. The red sweater I had bought for my sister went to his wife. I gave away two boxes of candy, the white mittens, and the leather gloves while my husband nodded approval.

And when I was breathless from reaching in and out of the car and the family stood there loaded with the gaiety of Christmas packages, the mother spoke for all of them. "We thank you," she said simply. And then she said, "Wait."

She hurried up the path to the house and came back with a quilt folded across her arms. It was beautifully handmade; the pattern was the Star of Bethlehem. I looked up at the tall beautiful pines because my throat hurt and I could not speak. It was indeed Christmas.

Every Christmas Eve since then, I sleep under that quilt, the Star of Bethlehem; and in my memory I visit the stable and smell again the corn shucks, and the meaning of Christmas abides with me once more.

UNDELIVERED GIFTS

WAYNE MONTGOMERY

Have you ever had the experience of almost not doing an act of thoughtfulness or charity—only to discover later that without this action on your part a very important experience would not have happened to someone else?

Whenever I am tempted to be lazy or indifferent in this way, I inevitably think back to that Christmas in Korea, in 1951.

It was late afternoon on December 24. After a cold, miserable ride by truck in the snow, I was back at our command post. Shedding wet clothing, I relaxed on a cot and dozed off. A young soldier came in, and in my sleep-fogged condition I heard him say to the clerk, "I wish I could talk to the Sergeant about this."

"Go ahead," I mumbled, "I'm not asleep."

The soldier then told me about a group of Korean civilians four miles to the north who had been forced to leave their burning village. The group included one woman ready to give birth. His information had come from a Korean boy who said these people badly needed help.

My first inner reaction was: How could we ever find the refugees in this snow? Besides, I was dead tired. Yet something told me we should try.

"Go get Crall, Pringle and Graff," I said to the clerk. When these soldiers arrived I told them my plan, and they agreed to accompany me. We gathered together some food and blankets; then I saw the box of Christmas packages in the corner of the office. They were presents sent over from charity organizations in the States. We collected an armful of packages and started out by Jeep.

After driving several miles, the snow became so blinding that we decided to approach the village by foot. After what seemed like hours, we came to an abandoned mission.

The roof was gone, but the walls were intact. We built a fire in the fireplace, wondering what to do next. Graff opened one of the Christmas packages in which he found some small, artificial Christmas trees and candles. These he placed on the mantel of the fireplace.

I knew it made no sense to go on in this blizzard. We finally decided to leave the food, blankets and presents there in the mission in the hope that some needy people would find them. Then we groped our way back to the command post.

In April 1952, I was wounded in action and taken to the hospital at Won Ju. One afternoon while I was basking in the sun, a Korean boy joined me. He was a talkative lad and I only half listened as he rambled on.

Then he began to tell me a story that literally made me jump from my chair. After he finished, I took the boy to our chaplain; he helped me find an elder of the local Korean church who verified the boy's story.

"Yes, it was a true miracle—an act of God," the Korean churchman said. Then he told how on the previous Christmas Eve he was one of a group of Korean civilians who had been wandering about the countryside for days after North Korean soldiers had burned their village. They were

nearly starved when they arrived at an old mission. A pregnant woman in their group was in desperate condition.

"As we approached the mission, we saw smoke coming from the chimney," the Korean said. "We feared that North Korean soldiers were there, but decided to go in anyway. To our relief, the mission was empty. But, lo and behold, there were candles on the mantel, along with little trees! There were blankets and boxes of food and presents! It was a miracle!"

The old man's eyes filled with tears as he described how they all got down on their knees and thanked God for their deliverance. They made a bed for the pregnant woman and built a little shelter over her. There was plenty of wood to burn and food to eat and they were comfortable for the first time in weeks. It was Christmas Eve.

"The baby was born on Christmas Day," the man said. He paused. "The situation couldn't have been too different from that other Birth years ago."

On the following morning American soldiers rescued the Koreans, who later became the nucleus of a Christian church in the village where I was recuperating.

You just never know when you have a special role to play in one of God's miracles.

CHAPTER SIX

ENTERING OUR LIVES AS STRANGERS

No ear may hear his coming,
But in this world of sin,
Where meek souls will receive him,
Still the dear Christ enters in.

N o room at the inn" has become a catchphrase to describe the plight of Mary and Joseph on Christmas Eve when they arrived in Bethlehem as strangers, looking for food and shelter. Though the innkeeper "had no room," we can credit him with providing some form of lodging for the Holy Family, getting them in out of the cold wind.

These days we are wary of strangers, with good reason. But over the centuries, hospitality—gracefully receiving friends and strangers—has become an important part of commemorating Christmas. The stories in this section describe encounters—at a restaurant, at residences, at a church—where strangers were welcomed. After the strangers left the scene, their presence seemed so mysterious and full of grace that their hosts wondered whether they had entertained heavenly beings, angels unaware.

— E.B.

CHRISTMAS IN THE GREENHOUSE

MARILYN FANNING

A greenhouse is a sanctuary in the winter, and sometimes Dad kept his nine greenhouses warmer than our own house right next door. Dad ran the family's third-generation flower business back in the 1930s in Utica, New York. Lilies, gladioli, mums and roses—he was known for his elaborate arrangements, lush and fragrant no matter what time of year. But perhaps the most beautiful of all were his Christmas poinsettias—velvety red, rosy pink and creamy white.

"Poinsettias are ornery plants," Dad always said, difficult to grow even under the best conditions. Because they preferred the warmth of the Southern sun to the frigid winter temperatures of central New York, Dad watched the weather extra close that time of year and spent a lot of time in the boiler room filling the cavernous furnace with heaps of coal. When the fire was good and hot, the pipes in all nine greenhouses hissed and crackled. They spewed steam that mingled with flower essence and earthen floor to produce a sweet, damp smell. I thought that must be what angels smelled like.

Dad stood outside the house one December day eyeing an ominous

sky. "Storm's coming," he said. At twelve years old I hadn't had enough experience to forecast the weather, but I did know his predictions were right. I went with him to the boiler room and checked the coal bin. "Plenty to last us," Dad said. He filled a wheelbarrow and carted it over to the furnace. "Stand back now, Marilyn," he said. He put all of his weight into each throw of the shovel to be sure the coal landed in the fire deep in the back of the furnace. This was backbreaking work, and Dad was strong from doing it. "We got to keep those delicate poinsettias so toasty they have no idea what's going on outside," he said.

By early evening, snow swirled around the greenhouse compound. Our windows at home were so frosty I could barely see out, but every now and then I'd get a whiff of that sweet dampness and know the fire and angels were keeping the poinsettias warm.

Cozy in my bed after dinner, I tried to sleep, but the wind rattling the windows woke me more than once. Then, in the dead of night, I heard my father pull on his boots and head out the back door. He always rose at 3:00 A.M. to do a coaling.

Dad didn't look so good at breakfast. By afternoon he coughed so bad he couldn't take more than a couple of steps before doubling over. After checking his temperature, Mother announced, "It's the grippe, Bill." She forbade him to go out to the greenhouses. "The hired men can get along without you for a day or two," she said, "and I'll see if somebody can stay the night." She made a mustard poultice for Dad's chest, which was about the only flu remedy in those days. At lunchtime, she brought him a bowl of broth and some bread, and delivered some bad news. "We're without help until this storm lets up," Mother said. "The roads are impassable, and it's too dangerous for the men to try to get here on foot."

"But who will coal the boilers?" Dad said. "We'll lose the poinsettias first, then everything will freeze!"

"Marilyn and I will just have to do it," Mother said.

"You can't!" My father coughed out the words. "You don't have the strength."

"We don't have a choice," Mother said. "Marilyn, bundle up."

Fighting our way through the heavy snow, we forced open the door to the boiler room. A full wheelbarrow of coal sat near the furnace. "Now we'll just pray," Mother said, "and God will give us the strength." Then she picked up a shovel. "You grab one too, and scoop as much coal as you can manage."

Both of us pitched our shovels into the black mound in the wheelbarrow. "You first," Mother said. I swung my shovel back and threw the coal with all my might. It went into the furnace opening—and that was about it. The coal was nowhere near close enough to the fire to do any good. Mother took her turn and grunted when she swung her shovel. But she didn't get much closer than I did.

We stared into the huge cave and at the small fire way in back. It seemed like a hopeless endeavor. "We must keep trying," she said. "Lord, please give us the strength we need." *How is the Lord going to do that?* I asked myself.

When we turned to fill our shovels again, we gasped in fright. A tall, husky man, dirty where he wasn't red from windburn, stood next to the coal bin.

"Maybe I can help," he said.

Mother put her arm protectively around my shoulders. "Where did you come from?" she asked, an edge to her voice.

"Ma'am, it's so cold outdoors, I came in here to get warm." The big man glanced into the furnace. "I can do that job for you," he said.

Practicality got the better of Mother's fear. "I'm sure you can," she said, sounding like my mother again. The man reached for my shovel, and I gladly handed it over. He jabbed it into the pile of coal and wielded that full shovel as if it were light as a feather, throwing right on target. The embers hissed. His next throw got the fire crackling again. Mother and I clapped.

"Our livelihood depends on the fire staying lit," Mother said. "I'd be more than grateful if you'd keep it going overnight, Mister—?"

"John," the man said. "Just John. You can be sure I'll keep it going. This feels like heaven to me."

"Are you hungry?" Mother asked.

"For now, keeping warm is the only thing on my mind." John settled in on a bench near the furnace.

"I'll be back in the morning with some food, and I hope you have a warm night's rest. You can wash up at the sink in the back room if you want," Mother said. "Good night. And thank you!"

Mother and I returned to the house to tell Dad the good news. "Wait till you see this man called John," Mother said. "He's over six feet tall and strong as an ox. Throws coal as well as you. He wandered into the greenhouse for shelter and I put him to work!"

"God knows I'm willing to help a guy who's down on his luck," Dad said. "But this time we're more helped than helping."

Mother laughed. "When I asked the Lord to send us strength, He did me one better and sent a strapping man to do the job."

By daylight, Mother had fixed a basket with a bowl of hot oatmeal, biscuits and jam, and apples from the fruit cellar. "You carry the towels and soap," she told me.

As we pushed open the greenhouse door, Mother exclaimed, "Oh, it's warm in here. We're going to be all right!"

John was sitting on a bench among the poinsettias and greeted us with a big smile. "Can you work another day?" Mother asked, handing him the basket and coffee. "We'll pay you for your work." John nodded and dug into his breakfast.

That day the storm subsided and Dad's fever broke. "Don't rush out to the greenhouses just yet," Mother said. "John's taking care of the coaling. Let's make sure you're well." She brought John lunch, and then dinner. The furnace were well tended.

"You know," Dad said that night, "maybe I could afford to hire another hand. I feel I owe that man something."

But when Dad dressed the next morning and went to the boiler room, John wasn't there. On the bench, neatly folded, lay the towels. The dinner dishes had been rinsed and stacked in Mother's basket. "John's gone," Dad told us at the house.

"A hobo gone without the pay he was due? How can that be?" Mother asked.

"You said yourself the Lord sent him, Mildred. Maybe there's more truth in that than you realized. All I know is, the good man's gone."

With the storm gone as well, business resumed. The regular workers returned and customers descended on us once more. Christmas was only two weeks away, and that year Dad's poinsettias were more beautiful than ever, the flowers extra large and the leaves a vibrant green. I walked among them, admiring them, the steam hissing and crackling in the pipes, releasing the sweet smell of greenhouse angels.

GUESS WHO'S COMING
TO DINNER

SUNNY MARIE HACKMAN

My son Victor, coming home from college, called from the bus station on Christmas Eve. "Could I bring a guest for dinner?" he asked. "I met this guy on the bus. He's hoping to surprise his family. He hasn't seen them for five years."

I was speechless. Didn't Vic know how carefully I'd planned this night? I didn't want a stranger at our family table!

Vic's guest was a man in his thirties with longish hair. "Thanks for having me," John said. Vic showed him to the telephone. He left a message for his family. *What if he's here all night?* I worried.

Dinnertime conversation was strained. I couldn't help wishing John would be on his way, and I'm sure he knew it. We went into the living room. I glanced at my guitar propped up by the piano. "Do you play an instrument?" I asked John.

"Sure do." John picked up the guitar and played "O Come, All Ye Faithful." He moved to the piano for "Amazing Grace" and "Jesus Loves Me." Now this felt like Christmas.

"That was my gift to you," John said.

I got out the camera and took a great shot of everyone with John. The doorbell rang. I was almost sorry John's family had come to get him so soon. *He's an angel in disguise*, I thought as we said good-bye.

A week later I picked up the roll of film from our Christmas Eve. John didn't appear in a single shot—as if he wasn't there at all.

STRANGER
AT TABLE FIVE

CORYNE WONG-COLLINSWORTH

It was five days before Christmas, and the café where I worked in northern California glowed with strands of red and green chili peppers. Holiday music played over the sound system and my co-workers excitedly discussed their plans. "Doing anything special?" they asked me. I shook my head no.

I was three thousand miles from my family in Hawaii, pursuing my lifelong dream of becoming a pediatric nurse. I attended classes all day, then went straight to my full-time waitress job at night. My weekly schedule left me exhausted and extremely homesick.

I had always looked forward to the holidays. But this December I felt unable to go on. In my prayers I told God that if I could just get home to see my mom, dad and brothers, I could survive the next two years until I graduated. But how? Rent, tuition, textbooks and other expenses left me with no extra cash. Money to go home? I barely had money to eat.

"I'm on my break. Cover for me, will you?" asked Maribelle, another waitress, as she passed me on her way to the employees' lounge. "By the way, there's this guy at table five," she said. "He's been sitting there for

more than an hour, not making any trouble but not ordering anything either." She paused. "It's like he's . . . waiting for somebody."

I looked in the corner. Sure enough, there was a slim, pleasant-looking man dressed in worn Levis, a red-and-black plaid shirt, and a black baseball cap, just sitting, alone. I went over, trying to muster a smile. "I'm Cory," I said. "Please let me know if you want anything."

I was turning to walk away when the man spoke. He had a soft, low voice, but somehow I could hear it clear and plain in the noisy restaurant. "I'd like an order of nachos," he said. "And a glass of water."

My heart sank. The nachos were the cheapest thing on the menu, which meant I wouldn't get much of a tip. But maybe this guy was broke, and I sure knew how that felt. So I tried my best to make him feel okay. "Coming right up," I said. I returned a few minutes later and slid the nachos in front of him. "That will be two dollars and ninety-five cents."

He reached into his pocket and handed me a single bill. "Keep the change," he said quietly.

I looked—then looked again. "Excuse me, sir," I said. "This is a hundred-dollar bill."

"I know," he replied gently.

My eyes opened wide. "I don't understand," I said. "What do you want from me?"

"Not a thing," he said, looking straight into my eyes. He stood up. "Call your mother tonight," he said. "Merry Christmas." Then he moved off in the direction of the front door. When I turned to thank him, he was nowhere in sight, although the exit was at least fifty feet away.

The rest of the evening passed in a blur. I finished work, went back to my apartment and put the money on the table. I had just turned on the television when the phone rang. It was my mother! She announced that my brothers had bought an airline ticket to get me home for Christmas. But they could only afford the fare one way. "Can you possibly manage the other part of the ticket?" she asked.

At that moment a commercial flashed on television. A major airline was announcing cut-rate fares to Hawaii, one way for ninety-nine dollars! I jumped off the sofa, shouting, "Thank You, God. I'm going home!"

Because of that visit to my family, I returned to my studies filled with new spirit and determination. Today I'm a registered nurse, caring for sick children. And every Christmas my husband John and I try to do something for someone else, just as the man at table number five had done for me. One year we purchased packages of warm socks and, with the wind howling at our backs, crept along the creek and handed them out to the people without homes who resided on the banks. The following Christmas we organized a blanket drive, and as the homeless gathered around a campfire, wrapped in their new blankets, John asked each to reflect on the tiny babe whose birthday it was.

Whether creeping along creek beds, tiptoeing down hospital corridors to hang stockings, or secretly leaving gifts of food (who knows where this Christmas will find us?), I always think of the mysterious stranger who helped me.

In my time of need he appeared—no halo or sparkling wings, but a sort of angel just the same. And that is the kind of angel we all can be.

THE MIRACULOUS
STAIRCASE

ARTHUR GORDON

On that cool December morning in 1878, sunlight lay like an amber rug across the dusty streets and adobe houses of Santa Fe. It glinted on the bright roof of the almost completed Chapel of Our Lady of Light and on the nearby windows of the convent school run by the Sisters of Loretto. Inside the convent, the Mother Superior looked up from her packing as a tap came on her door.

"It's another carpenter, Reverend Mother," said Sister Francis Louise, her round face apologetic. "I told him that you're leaving right away, that you haven't time to see him, but he says . . ."

"I know what he says," Mother Magdalene said, going on resolutely with her packing. "That he's heard about our problem with the new chapel. That he's the best carpenter in all of New Mexico. That he can build us a staircase to the choir loft despite the fact that the brilliant architect in Paris who drew the plans failed to leave any space for one. And despite the fact that five master carpenters have already tried and failed. You're quite right, Sister; I don't have time to listen to that story again."

"But he seems such a nice man," said Sister Francis Louise wistfully, "and he's out there with his burro, and. . . ."

"I'm sure," said Mother Magdalene with a smile, "that he's a charming man, and that his burro is a charming donkey. But there's sickness down at the Santo Domingo pueblo, and it may be cholera. Sister Mary Helen and I are the only ones here who've had cholera. So we have to go. And you have to stay and run the school. And that's that!" Then she called, "Manuela!"

A young Indian girl of twelve or thirteen, black-haired and smiling, came in quietly on moccasined feet. She was a mute. She could hear and understand, but the Sisters had been unable to teach her to speak. The Mother Superior spoke to her gently: "Take my things down to the wagon, child. I'll be right there." And to Sister Francis Louise: "You'd better tell your carpenter friend to come back in two or three weeks. I'll see him then."

"Two or three weeks! Surely you'll be home for Christmas?"

"If it's the Lord's will, Sister. I hope so."

In the street, beyond the waiting wagon, Mother Magdalene could see the carpenter, a bearded man, strongly built and taller than most Mexicans, with dark eyes and a smiling, wind-burned face. Beside him, laden with tools and scraps of lumber, a small gray burro stood patiently. Manuela was stroking its nose, glancing shyly at its owner. "You'd better explain," the Mother Superior said to Sister Mary Helen, "that the child can hear him, but she can't speak."

Good-byes were quick—the best kind when you leave a place you love. Southwest, then, along the dusty trail, the mountains purple with shadow, the Rio Grande a ribbon of green far off to the right. The pace was slow, but Mother Magdalene and Sister Mary Helen amused themselves by singing songs and telling Christmas stories as the sun marched up and down the sky. And their leathery driver listened and nodded.

Two days of this brought them to Santo Domingo Pueblo, where the sickness was not cholera after all, but measles, almost as deadly in an Indian village. And so they stayed, helping the harassed Father Sebastian, visiting the dark adobe hovels where feverish brown children tossed and fierce Indian dogs showed their teeth.

At night they were bone-weary, but sometimes Mother Magdalene found time to talk to Father Sebastian about her plans for the dedication of the new chapel. It was to be in April; the Archbishop himself would be there. And it might have been dedicated sooner, were it not for this incredible business of a choir loft with no means of access—unless it were a ladder.

"I told the Bishop," said Mother Magdalene, "that it would be a mistake to have the plans drawn in Paris. If something went wrong, what could we do? But he wanted our chapel in Santa Fe patterned after the Sainte Chapelle in Paris, and who am I to argue with Bishop Lamy? So the talented Monsieur Mouly designs a beautiful choir loft high up under the rose window, and no way to get to it."

"Perhaps," sighed Father Sebastian, "he had in mind a heavenly choir. The kind with wings."

"It's not funny," said Mother Magdalene a bit sharply. "I've prayed and prayed, but apparently there's no solution at all. There just isn't room on the chapel floor for the supports such a staircase needs."

The days passed, and with each passing day Christmas drew closer. Twice, horsemen on their way from Santa Fe to Albuquerque brought letters from Sister Francis Louise. All was well at the convent, but Mother Magdalene frowned over certain paragraphs. "The children are getting ready for Christmas," Sister Francis Louise wrote in her first letter. "Our little Manuela and the carpenter have become great friends. It's amazing how much he seems to know about us all. . . ."

And what, thought Mother Magdalene, *is the carpenter still doing there?*

The second letter also mentioned the carpenter. "Early every morning he comes with another load of lumber, and every night he goes away. When we ask him by what authority he does these things, he smiles and says nothing. We have tried to pay him for his work, but he will accept no pay. . . ."

Work? What work? Mother Magdalene wrinkled up her nose in exasperation. Had that softhearted Sister Francis Louise given the man permission to putter around in the new chapel? With firm and disapproving hand, the Mother Superior wrote a note ordering an end to all such unauthorized activities. She gave it to an Indian pottery-maker on his way to Santa Fe.

But that night the first snow fell, so thick and heavy that the Indian turned back. Next day at noon the sun shone again on a world glittering with diamonds. But Mother Magdalene knew that another snowfall might make it impossible for her to be home for Christmas. By now the sickness at Santo Domingo was subsiding. And so that afternoon they began the long ride back.

The snow did come again, making their slow progress even slower. It was late on Christmas Eve, close to midnight, when the tired horses plodded up to the convent door. But lamps still burned. Manuela flew down the steps, Sister Francis Louise close behind her. And chilled and weary

though she was, Mother Magdalene sensed instantly an excitement, an electricity in the air that she could not understand.

Nor did she understand it when they led her, still in her heavy wraps, down the corridor, into the new, as-yet-unused chapel where a few candles burned. "Look, Reverend Mother," breathed Sister Francis Louise. "Look!"

Like a curl of smoke the staircase rose before them, as insubstantial as a dream. Its base was on the chapel floor; its top rested against the choir loft. Nothing else supported it; it seemed to float on air. There were no banisters. Two complete spirals it made, the polished wood gleaming softly in the candlelight. "Thirty-three steps," whispered Sister Francis Louise. "One for each year in the life of Our Lord."

Mother Magdalene moved forward like a woman in a trance. She put her foot on the first step, then the second, then the third. There was not a tremor. She looked down, bewildered, at Manuela's ecstatic, upturned face. "But it's impossible! There wasn't time!"

"He finished yesterday," the Sister said. "He didn't come today. No one has seen him anywhere in Santa Fe. He's gone."

"But who was he? Don't you even know his name?"

The Sister shook her head, but now Manuela pushed forward, nodding emphatically. Her mouth opened; she took a deep, shuddering breath; she made a sound that was like a gasp in the stillness. The nuns stared at her, transfixed. She tried again. This time it was a syllable, followed by another. "Jo-sé." She clutched the Mother Superior's arm and repeated the first word she had ever spoken. "José!"

Sister Francis Louise crossed herself. Mother Magdalene felt her heart contract. José—the Spanish word for Joseph. Joseph the Carpenter. Joseph the Master Woodworker of . . .

"José!" Manuela's dark eyes were full of tears. "José!"

Silence, then, in the shadowy chapel. No one moved. Far away across the snow-silvered town Mother Magdalene heard a bell tolling midnight. She came down the stairs and took Manuela's hand. She felt uplifted by a great surge of wonder and gratitude and compassion and love. And she knew what it was. It was the spirit of Christmas. And it was upon them all.

THE STRANGER

KERSTIN BACKMAN

I t was Christmas Eve twenty years ago, the very first Christmas we spent in our small, red wooden farmhouse on the outskirts of a forest in the north of Sweden. The place was old and very old-fashioned but so cheap that we could afford it. It had a small stable where we could keep a few horses and two small fields for the horses to run in. A narrow road led out to the main road. We were so far from the closest town that ours was always one of the last roads to be cleared of snow.

This Christmas seemed magical to us. Our family had never lived in the country before. Snow had been falling for days and the whole world was white and soft with downy snow. The neighborhood looked like a frozen sea with giant, white frozen waves. Late on that day, the snow stopped falling and the clouds vanished slowly. Pale sunshine from the sinking sun was reflected in sparkling cascades on the snow. The birches and pine trees in the forest were furry with snow.

It was like living in one of those glittering Christmas cards, and we were childishly happy in the silent whiteness. This winter seemed like a special gift made exclusively for us. Along with my husband and our two young children, I felt that this was a Christmas when anything could happen.

We had our traditional Christmas dinner late in the day, gathered around our old kitchen table. It was a traditional Swedish holiday dinner—a big ham, ribs, cabbage and peas, served with breads, cheeses and sausages of all kinds. Afterward we sat talking together in the flickering candlelight in the small sitting room and ignored the piles of dirty dishes in the kitchen.

Just then—at half past ten on a pitch-dark Christmas night—someone pounded on our front door.

We looked at each other around the table. We did not yet know any of our new neighbors, and of our old friends, who could possibly be dropping in on us, given that we lived so far from town? Another knock sounded. I got up and went to see who it was.

There in the snow, quite alone and with a sparkling, star-studded sky shining behind him, stood a complete stranger. On this cold Swedish night he wore no hat. His soft blond hair formed a halo around his head, his breath grew like a cloud out of his half-open mouth, and a pair of big eyes shone in a very pale face.

I stared at him. Then I looked out into the yard beyond him to see if anyone was with him. The yard was empty. All I could see were the deep, black holes in the snow that marked his path up to the front door.

He just stood there as I looked at him, his hands in his pockets, watching me. At last he spoke.

"Excuse me, ma'am, but have you got a television set?"

His question was so unexpected that I did not quite know what to say.

"Ah well, yes . . . yes we have," I said.

"Could you possibly let me watch a television program? I think there is one I'd like to see." His voice was soft and friendly. I stood silent. My first thought was that I must say no in the politest way possible. But although my mind thought of refusal, my tongue refused to say no. Deep inside I seemed to hear the voice of my pious old grandfather telling me, "The Christmas night is holy. You must never turn anyone away from your house that night, for if you do you are turning away Christ."

"Well . . ." I said slowly, trying to think of what to do. "What program would that be?"

"I don't remember," he said, "but if you will let me look in the newspaper I will tell you which one."

"Maybe you had better come in," I said, and opened the door the rest of the way.

The young man walked up the three steps and held out his hand for a firm handshake. He did not say what his name was and I did not ask. His hand was icy cold and I quickly saw the reason why. He had no mittens on. He was dressed in a worn gray trench coat buttoned up to his chin and he wore big rubber boots. Not much to wear on a cold winter night, I said to myself.

His eyes were blue like the summer sky, and when he smiled, I was surprised to see the trust in his eyes and on his face. I got the distinct feeling that he had been certain that I would let him in.

I invited him into the warm kitchen. As he stepped into the room, he caught sight of the food still spread on the table.

"Oh," he said quietly. "You have eaten, I see."

I was surprised to hear myself say, "Maybe you would like to taste some Christmas food?" By then my husband and children had joined us in the kitchen. None of them asked for an explanation of the stranger's presence. I had let him in and that was enough for them. The blond man smiled at them and shook their hands, still calm and trusting as a kitten.

Then he turned to the wood fire range and rubbed his hands together to warm them, glancing over at the dinner table while he stood there. "Yes," he said, in answer to my question. "If you have enough food, it would be very nice."

I relit the candles while the stranger walked around the table looking into the bowls and pots. He seemed unfamiliar with most of the dishes, and when he came to the red cabbage, he stopped and his eyes grew wide.

"But what is this?" he exclaimed. "It is quite black! Is there *blood* in it?"

"No," I assured him. "Red cabbage always turns black when you cook it in an iron pot."

"How strange," he muttered. "Perhaps I won't eat it."

Ham and bread, green cabbage and Christmas sausage, spareribs and peas, he tasted everything slowly and with a look of great concentration.

My little daughter stood close to me, staring quietly while he ate. At last our Christmas guest got up, thanking me for the feast. "If I may borrow the newspaper, I would like to check on the television programs." He got it and started reading while my daughter's eyes followed him, round and thoughtful. "Let's see, how about this show here?"

I looked over his shoulder at the TV guide. "It is too late for that one, was that the one you wanted to see?"

"I do not know," he said. "But this one, look! I am sure that this one is good. I would very much like to see it." He stepped into the little room where our television stood, pulled a chair from near the wall, and planted himself in front of the set. "Now then," he said. "How do you switch this on?"

His words sounded a bit solemn and his strange blue eyes were as eager as a child's, a child expecting a glorious treat.

We switched the set on for him and the whole family sat down to join him. A comedy was just starting, a funny story of the kind that the whole family can watch, even very young children. The stranger did not look at us while the television was on. He followed the story closely, and when the action grew frantic, he threw his head back and laughed so that his angel's hair flew around him.

The film had a happy ending. My husband reached over and snapped off the set. The night was silent outside the house. The stranger was still laughing quietly to himself. "Just imagine," he said softly. "Today I have even laughed."

He turned in his chair and looked at us, still with laughter in his cheeks. He looked carefully at each one of us as if he wanted to remember our faces. We all sat silently for a few minutes.

"Where are you going?" my husband asked.

"To Copenhagen," was his answer. "I come from the north of Sweden and I am going there to save people. There is so much sin there and the people need help."

"How do you travel?" my husband asked again. "By car?"

"No. I walk."

Had he walked the seven hundred or eight hundred miles from the north of Sweden to our house in the woods? And was he planning to walk the hundreds of miles south to Denmark too?

The words hung in the air. The stranger smiled and laughed once again with his strange and carefree tone. "Sometimes kind people give me a ride, sometimes I walk, sometimes I get food, and tonight I have even laughed." His blue eyes twinkled in genuine joy as if he had been given a grand gift.

He and my husband went on talking about this and that for a little while as I sat wondering what to do with our strange guest.

Our daughter pulled at my skirt and whispered, "Mum, is he going to spend the night here?"

I shook my head, quite at a loss. It was the stranger himself who solved the problem. Suddenly he got up and announced that he really must be going.

"Are you really going to . . . walk?" I asked. "There are no people on the roads tonight and the next town is far away."

"I'll be fine," he said, calmly.

He had this strange smile. It was not polite, not embarrassed. It broke out spontaneously as if he could not hold it back, an eager smile. It seemed as if he were looking forward to something we did not know or as if he had seen something we could not see.

Without thinking, I took a big orange from the fruit bowl and handed it to him. "Here, at least you will have something to eat while you are walking."

His smile broke out again. He took the orange and held it in his hand like a king holding his orb. "Imagine," he said reverently. "This orange has traveled all the way around the world to Sweden and now I am holding it in my hand. Is that not fantastic?"

Suddenly we all saw the orange with his eyes—a fantastic ripe orange from a warm country far, far away—and we too marveled at the sight.

He put the orange into his pocket. His hands were warm when he shook ours.

The Christmas night was absolutely still, cold and clear. The moonlight poured down over the sparkling whiteness and the lonely stranger, who took big steps in the deep snow. His footprints looked like black holes and his shining blond hair was the last we saw of him as he disappeared between the trees on his way back to the main road.

We watched him quietly, and then turned to go back into our warm house. It was my daughter who spoke first.

"Was that Jesus?" she asked.

I smiled an adult's smile. "No, it was not. You know, it is a very long time since Jesus was born on Christmas."

"I know!" she said impatiently. "But he can come whenever he wants to, can't he? I think that was Jesus!"

The next morning, on Christmas Day, we tried to follow the stranger's deep footprints toward the main road. But suddenly, we had to stop. Right there, in the middle of our own little path out to the road, the footprints suddenly ceased. We looked all around us at the pure untouched snow. No footprints, no car tire marks, absolutely nothing.

When we came to know our neighbors in the following months we always asked if they had seen a stranger walking alone on the road that Christmas Eve. No one had seen any sign of a stranger.

We never learned who the stranger was, or how he disappeared. But we cannot help wondering. . . .

CHAPTER SEVEN

SHOWING MERCY TO CHILDREN

Where children pure and happy
Pray to the blessed Child,
Where misery cries out to thee,
Son of the mother mild. . . .

This "children's" verse of "O Little Town of Bethlehem" is rarely printed in hymnbooks. But it reminds us that Phillips Brooks wrote this song for the young students in his parish Sunday school, youngsters in his care learning the basics of faith, the meaning of right and wrong, and the power of prayer.

The Christmas angel stories in this section mirror the mercy shown to Jesus as a child. Ilene Smith tells of an intervention that met the dire physical needs of some impoverished boys. The remaining stories are examples of angelic rescue and protection.

I can just imagine Mary and Joseph echoing the comment made by Ilene Smith in her "New Shoes for Christmas": "You just never do know where angels are going to appear," looking out for the little ones that are precious in their sight.

—E.B.

NEW SHOES
FOR CHRISTMAS

ILENE SMITH

After I graduated from high school I took my first year of college at a small institution in the foothills of New York State's Catskill Mountains. When Christmas approached, I went into a local department store to spend some hard-earned babysitting money for family gifts. And here I noticed a little episode that still makes me glad today, about forty-five years later.

A farmer had come in with his two boys, about seven and ten years of age, and was inquiring of a very supercilious young salesman about new shoes for his boys. They were to be Christmas presents, he carefully explained.

I knew that life could be pretty hard back on the small subsistence farms in the hills, and there was usually a discouraging shortage of cash. The three were not well dressed. Their overalls and jackets were shabby and had been worn so thin in places that some neat patching had been done in an attempt to hold the garments together. Also there was a penetrating odor of "barn" about them.

In those days the stables had to be shoveled out by hand. The manure

was heaped in a big pile by the barn to be spread over the fields when the weather was right or when there was time. (A little of this aging manure mixed into some ordinary dirt was the secret of the spectacular, colorful geraniums that many a hill housewife kept in her kitchen windows.) Indoor plumbing and running water were uncommon. Baths and laundering were not embarked upon lightly. And so it is not surprising that sometimes the aroma of sheep and cows, calves and chickens clung to those responsible for their care.

The salesman looked over his would-be customers, barely subduing a sneer, and asked what sizes the boys took. The father didn't know—just a larger size than what they had, which were broken down, scuffed, had holes in them, and were too small. The salesman, raising an eyebrow and winking at a co-worker, said, "Well, we don't have anything to fit them." "You don't?" asked the father anxiously, "but there's all those shoes over there," and he pointed at endless boxes of shoes on the shelves. "We don't have anything to fit them," the salesman repeated and, as the discouraged little group turned to leave, he held his nose mockingly so the other store personnel could see how offensive the good earthly odors of the barn were to him.

This whole episode left me heartsick, and I must admit that I wished various calamities might occur to the salesman, and soon. But I could not think of anything to do to set matters right.

The shoe affair was not over, however, as I had not been the only one to notice this little family and their shopping problems. A very stout woman, with a cane, a plain black cloth coat, and a velvet pillbox hat jammed down over her ears shouted sternly to the errant clerk, "George, how about these shoes right here—seems as though they'd be just right for

these little guys. All sizes, too—you'll never get anywhere in this business, George, if you don't learn your stock and MIND THE STORE, as I always told my late husband, who, if I do say so, had the best meat market in town. Reminds me, we're having boiled New England dinner at the Franklin House tonight. Plenty for those who've put in a good day's work, not much though for slackers." This was a serious threat to George, who ate at her boarding house. I later learned that there was always a long waiting list of people who wanted to take their meals at her establishment.

The woman managed to get George actually anxious to locate sturdy, well-fitting shoes for the boys. After the shoes were selected, boxed and tied up with stout string, she escorted the man and his boys over to a rack of warm, winter jackets. She said she had just happened to notice that they had been drastically marked down in what she called a pre-Christmas sale, fixing George with a flinty stare. George hastily agreed that this was correct. In the end, the father, with a pleased look on his thin tired face, and the boys, carefully carrying their purchases, started out the door. Just then, the lady puffed up to them and dropped a bag of old-fashioned chocolate drops with creamy vanilla centers into one of the sacks. "Little extra, from Santa Claus," she intoned severely. "See that you have a good Christmas now!"

"Well," I thought, "you just never know where angels are going to appear!" I was at a skeptical age and didn't exactly believe in angels! I had certainly never thought of an angel as being a heavy-set, tightly corseted middle-aged lady, red-faced with work-worn hands and overbearing manner, and hair marcelled in a way that was out of style even back then. And certainly not in a crowded department store full of tired, snappish Christmas shoppers (and clerks). But there it was—my own eyes had seen one.

In the years since, I have seen some other angels. They, too, were quite a revelation to one who had always envisioned them as having flowing robes, gauzy wings and carefully balanced halos! But even though they did not fit into my fanciful notion of angels, they always managed to bring peace, happiness and love into some situations that appeared dead-ended.

ROUTINE RUN

MIGUEL GUTIERREZ

I drive a truck and travel regularly from Fresno to Los Angeles, where I deliver flour to a macaroni company. Normally I leave about 2:00 A.M., when traffic is not so heavy. Then I get back home in time for lunch. My wife Mati wants all the family to eat together. With a newborn son and our three other children, Mati has her hands full, but still she likes us gathered round the big wooden table in the kitchen. What a Christmas this is going to be!

So on December 23, 1997, I decide to leave soon after the children go to sleep, around 11:00 P.M. Leave early, get home early, I figure. Mati will be pleased to see me at the breakfast table on Christmas Eve.

Behind the wheel, I pray for a safe trip and go on my way. For ten years I have been driving a truck in California, and before that in Mexico. Driving and praying go together for me. When I look out at the wide open road, I remind myself of the good things God has put in my path: four healthy children, my beautiful wife, steady work, a comfortable home and the two weeks' vacation I'd just taken to help Mati while her belly was so big. I think, I am a rich man. And if that is not wonderful enough, God also gives each one of us an angel! Mine is with me in my truck as I pull into the factory in

L.A. I turn up the collar of my coat and zip it to my neck before stepping out into the cold.

Unloading takes some time. I finish up at about five in the morning, grab a tall cup of black coffee and settle back in my rig. I ask God for another safe trip home.

I do some talking to the guys on the CB. Just passing the time. Then I am rolling north along Highway I-5, staying in the far right-hand lane. That is the lane for the big trucks. My eyes move in a pattern: I check the road, my mirrors, the speedometer. I keep the needle at fifty-eight miles per hour, just under the speed limit. There is nothing else to look at along this route. No people, no houses, nothing.

Traffic picks up as the sky grows light over the Tehachapi Mountains. I glance in the mirrors, then watch the road as I top a rise. As I go over it, something interrupts my pattern of looking and I turn my head to the left to look out the window. Why? I don't know. But I see something on the shoulder. A child? My foot goes to the air brake and I pull into the break-down lane. I know it was a child!

Hissing for about two hundred feet, my rig finally shudders to a stop. I throw open the door and jump down from the cab. It's still cold outside, maybe thirty-five degrees.

At the first break in the traffic, I shoot across the four lanes and head back to where I saw the child. Running in the cold, I huff and puff and feel foolish. Maybe somebody is making a joke and leaves a doll on the side of the road. Maybe it isn't a child at all! But I cannot take that chance. The pavement shakes as the cars and trucks roar by, no one seeing what I think I saw.

And then there he is. A little boy about two years old, the age of one of my own kids. The boy is strapped in a car seat and looks up at me with big dark eyes. He is shivering in the cold, but he does not cry. Where is his mama? I wonder. "Don't worry, chiquito," I say to him. "You are okay now."

His little face wrinkles. "I take care of you," I say, and pick him up, car seat and all, and run back to my truck. With the boy safe in the warm cab, I call the highway patrol. Waiting for them to show up, I take the boy out of the car seat and hold him. I ask him questions, try to get him to talk to me, tell me what happened. But he has no words for this stranger. My two-year-old would be quiet too.

In ten minutes two police cars pull up behind us. The boy starts to cry. Maybe the sirens scare him. I hug my little friend. "Listen, chiquito, nothing bad will happen to you."

I tell the police all I know, and they assure me they will find out who the boy belongs to. We exchange phone numbers so I can find out what happens. The police leave with the boy, and I finish my drive home, about one more hour. Instead of eating breakfast, I tell Mati all about the boy and think how blessed we are that our children are safe. Then I go to sleep.

On Christmas Eve, I learn the whole story. A car was stolen from a woman at the airport. The thief did not know a boy was in a car seat in the back! After driving around L.A. drinking, the thief dumped the child on the side of the highway. Car seat and all. Nearly two hours later I saw the boy. The police caught the car thief, and the boy is safe with his mother.

The next few days I think a lot about the baby Jesus and my own newborn baby. And all the little children in the world who need us. I thank God I left early on my run that cold night. And that He chose me to help that boy. I still am not sure why I happened to look in that one split second to see him. I think maybe the angel riding next to me, she turned my head. Oh yes, what a Christmas for my family!

TEN PRECIOUS MINUTES

NELSON SOUSA

On December 19, 1979, my partner Ray and I were working as construction divers at a bridge site near Somers Point, New Jersey. Snow had begun to fall early, and by noon it had gotten so heavy we had to knock off work.

As we waded through parking-lot drifts, I noticed that my boss's car didn't have snow tires.

"Hey, John," I said to him, "why don't you let me drive you home? I don't think you'll make it with those tires."

John considered for a moment, then nodded. "Okay, Nelson, you might be right." But as he started toward my pickup, he stopped and turned back to his car. "Oh, I almost forgot," he said, reaching into its trunk. "Here's your spare dry suit I borrowed last month. I finally remembered to bring it back."

I was about to take the suit to our onsite trailer office where we store gear. But since it had some holes in it, I decided to take it home to repair. I threw it into the back of my pickup. It was the first time in my ten years of diving that I had traveled anywhere with one of these protective rubber suits. They were always stored at work.

The drive north through the snow was rough, stop-and-go all the way. What should have taken us one hour took over three. But we spent the time talking about Christmas and the toys we were buying our kids.

I didn't really mind going out of the way for John, but by the time we got to his turnoff it was past three o'clock. We turned into his street. A fire engine roared by and stopped at the end of the block. There was a big commotion down there.

"Oh, dear God, no . . ." John said. Ahead was an alarming tableau: a frozen pond, an ominous black hole in its center. Fire trucks with lights flashing and people crowding the bank. A woman squalling and weeping.

"Somebody must have fallen through the ice," Ray said.

I pulled the pickup over to the side, jumped out, grabbed my dry suit from the back, pulled it on and ran to the pond. Ray stumbled along behind me zipping me up.

A grim-faced firefighter told us that a six-year-old boy had walked out on the ice and fallen in. "But it's hopeless," he groaned, "the ice is too thin for us to get out there." Two men had already tried. Even a ladder laid on the ice didn't work. And the water was so cold that anyone falling into it would be shocked into unconsciousness in minutes.

"I'll try," I said. Someone tied a rope around my waist and I headed out, splintering the ice into shards as I beat my way through it. By the time I reached the hole where the boy had disappeared, my hands were bleeding from the exertion.

Icy water surged through the holes in the suit I was going to repair. I knew I had only a minute or two for a dive. Then I discovered I had left my heavy diver's belt back at the job. Without it to weigh me down, it

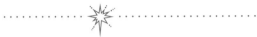

would be hard to swim underwater in my buoyant rubber suit. But I *had* to get down to the bottom.

All I could do was force my body down. The water looked black. About six feet down I touched the bottom, then bobbed up like a cork. Up and down, up and down I plunged, working partway around the opening in the ice frantically feeling for a body. But there was nothing, only frigid water and a slick muddy bottom. *Where was he?*

Gasping, coughing from exhaustion, I cried out in desperation: "He's not here! I can't find him. Where is he?"

Looking up across the pond, I saw a tall blond man in a light jacket standing by himself in the snow. He raised his arm and pointed to a spot on the side of the hole opposite me.

I pushed to the spot and thrust myself down. The ice-cold water closed over my head, and then my foot touched something. The boy's body! I surged up again. Now, with violent arm movements, I forced myself down and wrapped my feet around the body and drew it up. Floating on my back, I pulled the limp, sodden form across my chest and held him tight.

The little boy's soaked blue jacket seemed glued to him. I pulled back the hood covering his head and screamed. The pinched face was as blue as the jacket. He was not breathing. I could not look at him anymore.

"Pull me back!" I yelled, and the rope tightened around me as firefighters heaved on it, hauling me to the bank. John jumped into the water, took the form and passed it to waiting medics. I staggered upright, untied the rope and headed toward them when two policemen grabbed me. "C'mon," one urged, "get into our squad car and warm up."

"But the boy! . . ." I yelled. By now the ambulance's doors had

slammed shut and it sped away, siren wailing. I stood shaking my head, feeling helpless, wishing I could have saved him.

John, my boss, took me to his house where I warmed up some more, and then Ray and I drove home. When I walked in, my wife Patricia was preparing dinner. I didn't even kiss her, just stumbled over to the sofa and slumped down sobbing. It had all been so useless.

Pat looked at Ray. "Nelson pulled a little boy out of the pond," Ray explained.

Patricia had cooked my favorite dish, beef stroganoff, but I couldn't touch it. I could only sit on the living-room sofa thinking about that poor little fellow and how his parents were feeling.

Patricia called the hospital where the boy had been taken. They told her that little Michael Polukard had been underwater for around ten minutes. He was unconscious, in serious condition; a priest had given him last rites, but he was alive.

What a Christmas, I thought, staring into the glowing lights on our tree. Under it was our Nativity scene; the manger bed was empty—our custom is to place the Baby Jesus in it on Christmas Eve. I felt even worse thinking about a real little bed that was empty that night.

I looked gloomily around the room. On the TV set stood two white angels Patricia had made for the house that year. One held a string of stars, the other played a harp. How frivolous it all seemed now. Angels! I remembered how my Portuguese grandmother used to tell us kids about the angels who sang of Jesus' birth to the shepherds that long-ago night. But that night angels and Jesus didn't seem very real to me. And yet, my heart grieved so for the little boy that I did the only thing left for me to do. I leaned my head down and prayed for him. I asked God to help him live.

Hours passed as I sat, moodily staring at the wall. Patricia put our two little girls to bed and Ray tried to encourage me. "He's still alive, you know," Ray said. "There's hope. You should just be grateful that you knew where to find him in that pond."

I looked up. "I didn't know where he was, Ray," I said. "It was that big blond guy who pointed me to the right spot. If it hadn't been for him, I never would have found the boy."

Ray looked puzzled. "That's the strangest thing, Nelson. You keep talking about some guy on the other side of the pond but," he scratched his head, "there wasn't anybody over there."

About nine o'clock the phone rang. Patricia took it, then handed it to me. "It's Michael's father, he wants to thank you."

With shaking hand, I took the phone. "Don't worry about me," I blurted, "all I want to know is how your little boy is."

Stan Polukard said Michael was still in serious condition, but it looked as though he was going to make it. The very coldness of the water had slowed Michael's body functions, he explained, reducing his need for oxygen. I gave a big sigh of relief and, in my heart, thanked God for saving the little boy. Then I was able to fall into bed and sleep.

We kept in close touch with the hospital the following days, but the news wasn't good. The Polukards had been warned that Michael might have extensive brain damage. The doctors worried about all the time that had passed before his heart and lungs had resumed functioning. A test of his brain by an electroencephalogram had shown "inconclusive" results. Doctors said that only after he regained consciousness would they know how much he'd been damaged.

We learned that his mother and father moved into the hospital to stay with the boy. The news reported that they were praying for him around the clock. People everywhere sent encouraging messages, saying they were praying with them. I didn't know that there were that many strong believers.

The papers kept up a running account of Michael's plight. Eileen and Stan Polukard continued to talk to their little boy, who lay unconscious, connected to a respirator, a heart monitor and intravenous lines. The doctors tried to protect them from false hope.

"Remember," one doctor warned Eileen, "the child you knew may no longer exist."

On the third day, Friday, the medical staff took Michael off the respirator. Stan and Eileen continued their patient, prayerful vigil at their son's bedside. Suddenly, Michael began to stir. Then, opening his eyes, he slowly turned toward them. "Hi Mom, hi Dad," he whispered.

On Monday afternoon, Christmas Eve, we got a phone call.

"Michael's home!" my wife shouted. The Polukards had called saying that tests showed Michael completely well and normal and that they could take him home. They invited us to their house to celebrate with them.

Patricia and I bundled our two little girls into the car and hurried over.

Michael was dressed in pajamas and sitting on the living-room sofa when we came in. "Do you know who I am?" I asked. For the rest of the evening he wouldn't leave my side. And as we talked he happened to mention that one of the first things he saw when he opened his eyes in the hospital was an angel.

"An angel?" I said, surprised.

There had been an angel there, all right. A big paper angel had hung over Michael's bed as part of the hospital's Christmas decorations.

Angels again. Once more I thought of that mysterious time my grandmother used to tell us about when the angels spoke to the shepherds in the fields and told them about the little Baby lying in a manger.

I pictured our own little crèche in our living room at home. When we'd get back, our two little girls would place the Baby Jesus in His manger bed.

I glanced up and saw Michael in his father's arms and I gave thanks to the One Who had sent us His Son . . . and Who, I now knew for certain, sent His help, somehow, someway, so that another little bed would be warm tonight.

But there was another picture in my mind, a tall blond man standing alone in the snow beside the pond, pointing. Who was he? In all the weeks and months to come, I would find no one who had seen him there. On this happy Christmas Eve, in a room filled with quiet celebration, I couldn't help but wonder.

ANGEL IN THE HOUSE

BONNIE WILSON

By now the kids and I were used to Steve's being on the road. His trucker job sometimes kept him away for a month at a time. We were glad to have him home for Christmas, but just after New Year's he had to go again. Steve loved his job. But that didn't make it any easier for him to say good-bye.

"I think about you when I'm out there," he said as he hugged me at dawn that January morning. "I pray for God to watch over you all. Sometimes it doesn't feel like enough."

"Don't you worry yourself."

The kids and I quickly fell into our daily routine without Steve. But nights were another story. One cold Monday I got ready for bed. I imagined Steve driving along a stretch of roadway. I wished he was home with us instead.

I walked into the girls' room. Kimberly, ten, and Carrie, eight, were ready for bed. "How about I sleep in here tonight?" I asked.

"What about Ray?" said Carrie.

Their brother Ray's room was right next to the girls' with a connecting door between the two. Yes, Ray should be here with us.

What a strange thought. Ray was twelve, almost a teenager. He would not want any part of this.

Ask him.

I stuck my head through the doorway. Ray was sitting up in bed. "We're all sleeping in here tonight," I said. "Why don't you join us? Come on, it'll be fun."

Ray thought about it. "Okay," he said. "If you want."

"This is kind of nice, all of us together like this, isn't it?" I said as we settled in. The kids and I traded jokes and talked about what Steve might be doing. He'd called home earlier from a truck stop in Missouri. "Lord, keep him safe on the road," I asked. No matter where he was, I knew Steve's prayer was the mirror opposite of mine: "Lord, keep my family safe at home." I said good night to the kids and shut off the light.

It was still dark when I woke up. Someone was shaking me. "Kim?" I murmured. "Go back to sleep."

Kim shook me again and pointed at the open door to Ray's room. I sat up. I rubbed my eyes, straining to see. Something was in the doorway. What is that? In the dim light I could make out a tall figure, with wings? The figure had one hand on the door frame. The other motioned us out. An angel was telling us to leave the house. Why?

I craned my neck to look past the angel into Ray's room. The walls were alive with an orange glow. Fire? I couldn't see any smoke. I didn't smell smoke. But the room was definitely on fire. And then I realized: The angel was holding back the flames and smoke.

"Kids, wake up! We have to get out." The kids jumped out of bed, grabbed blankets, and we all hurried outside.

A policeman met us at the door. A fire truck came screaming up the

street. When I looked back at the house I saw the kids' bedrooms in flames. The windows exploded and the fire roared out. We barely made it, I thought.

The kids and I went to my parents' house, and I left word with Steve's trucking company about what had happened and where we were. "Thank goodness you were awake," my mom said as we got the kids settled down.

"Kim woke me," I said. "She pointed at—" I looked over at Kim, already asleep. Had she seen the angel too? Could I have imagined it? "Kim pointed at the fire," I finished.

Next morning we learned that the fire had started in the light switch on the porch, traveled up through the wires and burned through the wall in Ray's room. That's where the flames had first appeared. I drove over to take a look. The kids' rooms were gutted, the walls black and charred. The ceiling had burned away, leaving a few beams and the roof above it. Nothing was salvageable. Then I saw our Bible, the pages unburned. I took it with me when I left.

When I got back to my parents' house Kim was waiting to talk to me. "Mom?" she asked. "Did you see anything strange in our room last night when you woke up?"

My heart beat a little faster, but I didn't want to influence Kim's story with my own. "What did you see?"

"I think I saw an angel," Kim said, "standing in the doorway holding back the fire."

I gave Kim a hug. "I saw it too."

Steve drove home from Missouri without stopping. I threw my arms around him. "I'm just sorry I wasn't here to protect you. I meant to ask," he said, "what was Ray doing sleeping in the girls' room?"

I remembered my strange urge to ask Ray to sleep with us.

"Thank God," said Steve. "He heard my prayers."

Steve's back on the road now. But I sleep just fine. It's still hard for us to say good-bye, but Steve and I both know he doesn't have to be at home for us to be safe. Our prayers are always enough.

"I WASN'T LOST"

KAREN KINGSBURY

Austin Rozelle was four years old when his parents noticed his imagination truly taking wing. He loved sports, particularly basketball, and often pretended to be the greatest player of all, Michael Jordan. At bedtime when the Rozelles' children asked for favorite bedtime stories, Austin's request never changed.

"Tell me a Michael Jordan story, Daddy, please!"

And Burt Rozelle would make up a story involving Austin and Michael Jordan and some type of crucial basketball game. It got so that as Christmas approached that year, Austin wanted only one thing: a visit from Michael Jordan. Throughout the month of December, when the doorbell would ring at the Rozelle house, Austin would run toward the front door yelling, "It's probably Michael Jordan!"

So it was that three days before Christmas, a chilly, damp Sunday, when Austin dribbled his child-sized basketball into the family's Portland, Oregon, house and announced he was going to Michael's house, his mother thought nothing of it. Austin was always pretending to be visiting with Michael Jordan or taking a trip to his house. Austin tugged on his mother's skirt while she washed the dishes. "Bye, Mom. I'm going to see Michael Jordan."

Stella Rozelle smiled at the child. "Okay, Austin, have fun."

Obviously Austin had no idea where Michael Jordan lived, nor the truth that he did not live in Oregon. Even if he had known the exact location, Stella knew the boy would never really leave the house. Especially by himself. Austin was merely playing a game of make-believe, as he had so many other times, and Stella felt at ease as she continued her conversation and watched the child disappear into the backyard.

Fifteen minutes later Stella finished the dishes and sauntered outside to round up Austin and his six-year-old brother Daniel. The older child was swinging on the family swingset, happily humming a tune from Sunday school earlier that day. The temperature was dropping, and Stella wanted the children to come inside before they caught cold.

"It's getting too cold out here, buddy. Let's go inside and have some dinner." She stood up and glanced around the yard. "Where's Austin?"

Daniel shrugged as he jumped off the swing. "He was dribbling his ball and he went out that way." Daniel pointed down the street. "He told me he was going to see Michael Jordan."

Suddenly Stella's blood ran cold as she remembered a billboard she'd forgotten until now. It was two miles away on Martin Luther King Boulevard and it had a larger-than-life photograph of Michael Jordan. "Daniel, you don't think he's going to that billboard picture of Michael Jordan, do you?"

Daniel thought for a moment and then shrugged. "Probably. He told me once that he thinks Michael lives there."

Stella's heart was immediately in her throat. She ran in the house, found Burt in the computer room and explained the situation.

"You can't find him anywhere?" Burt's face immediately drained of all its color.

She felt panic welling within her and she shook her head. "He's gone, Burt. Pray. Please pray."

Stella called a neighbor to come stay with Daniel and she and Burt searched the house and yard again.

"What's the last thing you remember him saying or doing?" Burt asked as they climbed into the car and set off slowly down the street, straining to see into every yard.

Stella ran her fingers nervously through her hair. "I was washing dishes, getting ready for dinner, when Austin came in with his ball and told me he was going to see Michael Jordan."

"He says that all the time."

"Exactly. I thought he was just playing and I said okay."

Burt rounded the corner as the two of them exchanged a terrified look. Thirty minutes had passed since Austin's disappearance. If their son had attempted the two-mile walk to Martin Luther King Boulevard by himself, he could have been kidnapped or hit by a car. In addition, the weather report had forecasted snow and Austin wasn't dressed warmly enough for the near-freezing temperatures. Most frightening of all, he could be anywhere because the child was too young to have any sense of direction.

While Burt wove their car up and down the side streets leading toward the busy thoroughfare, Stella used their cell phone to call the police.

Burt continued to drive the streets near their house and Stella searched up and down each sidewalk as she waited for the police officer to take a full report. Every moment that passed meant that Austin could be getting picked up by a stranger or run over. She struggled to breathe, suffocated by the feeling of helplessness. Would they be forced to celebrate Christmas without finding Austin? Would they be making funeral plans?

On the verge of hysteria, she covered her face with her hands and began to pray. Suddenly the story of baby Jesus came to mind—the ways in which King Herod tried to have the Christ child killed. On every turn angels were there to protect Jesus. "Please, God . . ." she prayed out loud. "Please watch over Austin and lead me to him. Put Your Christmas angels around him, wherever he is."

Nearly an hour after the boy had disappeared and more than a mile from their house, they turned onto a busy street one block from Martin Luther King Boulevard and saw a foursome on the sidewalk half a block ahead. Two tall, slim, dark-haired women and a younger, blonde woman were walking together a few feet behind a boy with blond hair wearing a red and black sweatshirt and black sweatpants. The child was carrying a basketball.

"Austin!" Burt shouted. He sped up, pulling alongside the three women and little Austin and quickly parking the car. "Austin! Thank You, God. Thank you."

"Austin!" Stella shouted as she jumped out of the car and joined them. The women stood back and watched as Stella and Burt swept the little boy into their arms. Relieved and sobbing, Stella fell to her knees next to Austin and pulled him tightly to her, stroking his hair and closing her eyes.

"We thought we'd lost you, baby," she cried into his downy soft hair. "Thank You, God."

"I wasn't lost, Mommy. I was going to Michael Jordan's house!" Austin smiled easily, calm and unaffected by his adventure away from home.

Standing back, careful not to interrupt the reunion, the women who had been trailing behind the boy smiled.

"He's a character, that one," the older woman said softly. "He was chasing his ball and he fell into a ditch back there a ways. There was a bit of water in it and we helped him out. We've been following him ever since so he wouldn't get hurt."

Stella nodded, still clinging tightly to the child. "Thank you so much," she said, wiping at her tears and looking Austin over to be sure he was all right.

The woman continued. "He said he was going to Michael Jordan's house."

The other tall woman smiled. "Isn't he that professional basketball player?"

"Yes." Stella couldn't take her eyes from Austin, relieved and grateful beyond words that her son was unharmed.

"Does he live around here?" The older woman wrinkled her nose, clearly confused.

Burt shook his head and uttered a short laugh as he tousled Austin's hair. "Austin has quite an imagination lately." He looked at Stella. "I guess we didn't know exactly how much."

"Anyway," the woman said, "he seemed to know where he was going."

Stella nodded, paying little attention to the women. She swept the boy into her arms and thanked the women once more for their help. Then, fresh tears of relief streaming down her cheeks, she and Burt drove off to share the good news with the police and the others.

They were at the end of the street when Burt hit the brakes. "How thoughtless of me—I should have offered those women a ride home. It's freezing outside."

He did a U-turn and headed back down the block, but the women

were gone. Stella checked her watch. Not even two minutes had passed since they had left the women, but now as she and Burt looked up the street, there was no one in sight.

"That's strange," she muttered aloud. "No one could walk that fast. I wonder where they went."

Back at the house Stella and Burt ran inside with Austin in their arms. "We found him walking a mile from here. Three neighborhood women were walking behind him, watching out for him."

"Oh, thank You, dear Lord." The neighbor kissed Austin on the cheek and then left the Rozelles to themselves. By then Daniel had come into the room, awed by the fact that Austin had actually left and grateful that he was home safe. Burt and Stella put their arms around Austin, pulling him close once more as the family formed a circle.

"We were worried about you, Austin," Stella said softly.

"I know, Mommy. I won't go to Michael Jordan's house anymore. Next time he'll come here."

"That's good," Burt said.

Stella smiled and took the boy's cold damp hands in hers. "Listen, Austin, remember those ladies who helped you and stayed with you?"

The child nodded. "Yes, Mommy. They were strangers."

"But you weren't afraid of them, were you?"

"No, they were nice."

Burt nodded. "Yes, they looked after you. Did they tell you their names?"

"They told me they were from God," Austin said simply.

There was a pause as Stella, Burt and Daniel leaned closer, curious expressions on their faces.

"Oh yeah." Austin looked up at his mother. "What's an angel, Mommy?"

The adults stared at the child for a moment, and then exchanged a knowing look as goose bumps rose up on their arms. Quietly, and with a greater understanding than at any time in his life, Burt directed his family to hold hands; then he closed his eyes and bowed his head. When he spoke his voice was filled with awe.

"Dear God, we do not know Your ways and we do not pretend to have answers. But somehow today we know that You brought about divine intervention in the life of our little Austin. Thank You for hearing our prayers and bringing him home safely. And God—" Burt paused, his voice choked with emotion. "Thank You for the simple faith of our children.

"And thank You for Your Christmas angels."

CHAPTER EIGHT

OPENING THE DOOR TO FAITH

Where charity stands watching
And faith holds wide the door,
The dark night wakes, the glory breaks,
And Christmas comes once more.

In the middle of her story "The Glow Across the Field," Carmen Robertson faces a Christmas-morning crisis; she feels that "angels, peace on earth—they were all part of a fairy tale." But by Christmas night she sees things differently: "Christmas had come after all. I knew I would never again lose my faith in its promises of good will, of joyous surprises, of hope."

Carmen's story, and the others in this section, prompt us to believe . . . in the power of God . . . in the presence of His caring messengers, human and heavenly . . . and in the miracle that is Christmas itself.

As you turn the page, let faith open the door to Christmas. Let Christmas open the door to faith.

— E.B.

THE GLOW
ACROSS THE FIELD

CARMEN ROBERTSON

I sat at the kitchen table Christmas Eve morning staring out the window at the wide frozen field that separated our house from that of our neighbor Mrs. Houston. If only Daddy were home. This was the night he would set me on his lap and read to me about the angels that visited the shepherds on the first Christmas Eve. Then we'd look out across the field and pretend we saw angels in every shooting star and shadowy bird, even in the faint wisps of smoke curling up from Mrs. Houston's chimney. And we'd make believe that the cheery orange glow from her house was some shepherd's campfire.

But it was 1941 and Daddy was in the Army. We hadn't heard from him in weeks, and I was worried because of the news on the radio. Mother had taken work as a clerk to keep us fed and clothed. There was a sad weariness in her eyes that kept me from asking her to make divinity or gingerbread men. Instead I tried to make the cookies myself, but they came out sad-looking, too, with droopy raisin mouths and wrinkled brows.

We didn't even have a Christmas tree; my older brother Carson, who usually made a fuss over finding the perfect one, didn't seem to care. All that tough year I had looked forward to the magic of Christmastime. Yet now there was only gloomy emptiness. Perhaps the war raging in Europe had scared off even the imaginary angels.

"Carmen," my mother called from the couch. I went to her and she handed me a five-dollar bill. "Go to the store and buy each of us a present." She gave me a tired pat on the arm and returned to her mending.

I put on my coat and mittens and tucked the five-dollar bill into my pocket. I should have been excited that Mother was treating me as a grown-up. After all, at age eleven, I'd "known" about Santa Claus for some time. Still, I would have preferred the excitement of unwrapping a surprise gift.

I kept my mittened hand wrapped tightly around the money as I started out across the icy field toward the general store two miles away. The trees reached out their bare limbs to the stony sky. Mounds of snow remained at the bottom of old cornstalks. The wind whipped at my back, blowing my hair into my eyes. I started to think about what to get for Mother and Carson. Maybe they'd smile when they opened their gifts. Maybe we'd laugh and talk and sing carols. Maybe Christmas would feel like Christmas again.

A rabbit darted out from one of the clumps of snow into my path. Startled, I slipped and fell to the hard-packed ground. I got up and rubbed my knee, blinking back tears.

Through the trees I spied a curl of blue-gray smoke rising from Mrs. Houston's chimney. *She's probably making gingerbread cookies right now,* I thought. *Happy ones.* I remembered the time when, inspired by Daddy and our Christmas ritual, I had ventured close to her house to search for campfire ashes and sheep tracks. Mrs. Houston had come out, tall and

broad-shouldered, dressed in a crisp brown-and-white-checked pinafore. I froze, afraid she'd be mad. But she had looked at me with kind eyes and invited me in for some cookies and cocoa. "I'm so glad you came," she said, giving me a big hug as if she'd known me forever.

Standing there looking at her house now, with a knee that felt as though it had been skinned, and nose and ears numb from the cold, I wanted nothing more than to be sitting in her warm kitchen, eating Christmas cookies. Somehow it seemed that being with her would make everything cheerful again. But I had grown-up responsibilities and there wasn't time to dawdle. I hurried on.

In town, people carrying wrapped packages and sacks of groceries wished each other happy holidays. I ran up the steps to the general store. It smelled of cedar and oranges. Music played from a radio on the counter. I fingered scarves and neckties, sniffed at bottles of perfume, looked longingly at a basket of Brazil nuts. Five dollars would never be enough for all I wanted to buy. I dug my hand into my pocket. It was empty. The five-dollar bill! I checked my other pocket, whisked off my mittens to see if it had slipped into one of them. Nothing. Panic welled inside me.

Frantically I unbuttoned my coat and flung it to the floor, checked the pockets of my dress, then turned my coat pockets inside out. I ran around the store, checking under tables, on shelves, inside boxes, scarcely noticing the stares of other customers. Then I knocked over the basket of Brazil nuts. When the man behind the counter came over, I grabbed his arm. "My five-dollar bill! Have you seen it?"

He shook his head, bewildered. I ran out onto the store porch and asked everyone if they'd seen my money. A couple of people shook their heads sympathetically, saying, "Sorry, kid." Others shrugged as if to say "tough luck."

I finally went back inside the store. As the radio blared "Joy to the World," I replaced the scattered nuts. I picked up my coat and put it back on, buttoning it meticulously as if that would make up for my carelessness with the money. There was news about the war, then a song about angels singing. *I need an angel now*, I thought. I wiped the tears from my eyes, and slowly, methodically, began to retrace my steps home, searching for the money.

The sun had started to set, muted by a cluster of clouds. Wind stung my face. I squinted at Mrs. Houston's house in the distance and rubbed my smarting knee. That's it, I realized. I must have jerked my hand out of my pocket to catch myself when I fell. I followed the rabbit's tracks as far as they were visible. I should have been more careful, I chided myself. I had ruined everything.

The sunlight was fading rapidly now, the first evening star shining faintly. I had to go home. What had I been expecting—some Christmas miracle? An angel swooping down to make Christmas happy again? No tree. No gingerbread men. And now no gifts. Obviously God wasn't sending any angels either. I trudged home, feeling as if I had lost much more than a five-dollar bill.

I walked into the house and immediately confessed, "I lost the money," so ashamed I didn't care what my punishment would be. But Mother said nothing. Neither did Carson. I wished they would. Perhaps they'd given up on Christmas too. We barely spoke during dinner. After Mother and Carson had gone to their rooms, I stayed at the kitchen table alone in the dark. The distant glow from Mrs. Houston's house and the few weakly glittering stars did little to lighten the somber sky. I tried to imagine a shepherd's campfire, feel the awe I always felt when Daddy told the Christmas story, but I couldn't. Santa Claus, angels, peace on earth—they were all part of a fairy tale. I crept to bed.

The next morning I rolled wearily out from under my covers and went to the kitchen. Mother was heating water to wash some sheets. *Christmas is, after all, just another day*, I told myself. I looked out the window to see if the weather was all right for hanging the laundry. Bright sunshine reflected off the frost-covered field. A moving shape in the distance caught my attention and I watched it curiously. Soon I recognized Mrs. Houston. Was she coming over here? She'd never visited our house before.

"Mother, come look." She joined me at the window, then went to open the door.

"Merry Christmas," Mrs. Houston announced, setting a lumpy cloth sack on the linoleum floor. Mother started up the coffeepot and Carson took Mrs. Houston's coat. Beneath it she wore the same pinafore I remembered, the shoulder ruffles standing up stiffly like little wings.

Mrs. Houston removed three small packages from the bag and handed one to each of us. We stood there, speechless. Finally Mother cleared her throat and softly said, "We don't have anything for you."

"Your gift is just being here so I have someone to give to," Mrs. Houston replied, smiling. Suddenly our kitchen felt as warm as hers had that day I visited. "Now open your packages, all of you, and enjoy!"

For Mother there was a red can of Mavis talcum powder. Carson's gift was a comb and brush set. I carefully unwrapped the colorful paper from my box and smoothed out the ribbon, prolonging the moment. At last I took out a small brown purse with a gold-colored chain. I wouldn't lose another five-dollar bill, that was for sure.

Mother, eyes shining, looked at our guest and declared, "Mrs. Houston, you are an angel."

An angel? I turned to look at Mrs. Houston too. Yes, she must be. How else could she have known to come this particular Christmas? How else could it seem as if a fire had just been rekindled? "Won't you stay for a while?" Mother said to Mrs. Houston. "You can help me make the divinity."

Carson took the ax and went to chop down a cedar tree. I made paper chains for decoration. "Jingle Bells" played loudly on the radio, Mother and Mrs. Houston singing along as they took turns beating the egg whites. Christmas had come after all. I knew I would never again lose my faith in its promises of good will, of joyous surprises, of hope.

When Dad returned home a few months later, I told him all about our Christmas with Mrs. Houston. I climbed onto his lap and we gazed out across the field and shook our heads in wonder. We agreed that we had spent all those years imagining angels in the sky when there had been a real one right next door.

A VOICE CRYING IN THE CONGREGATION

DAVID MICHAEL SMITH

He staggered in fifteen minutes after the traditional holiday hymn sing had begun, plopping with a thud in the wooden pew directly behind me. It was Christmas Eve at historic St. Paul's Episcopal Church in the small and quaint town of Georgetown, Delaware, and midnight Mass was scheduled to commence in about twenty minutes. Dozens of candles cast a warm glow throughout the church. Accompanied by the pipe organist, the congregation joined the choir in a unified voice of celebration and joy.

I recall smelling the strong odor of alcohol right behind me. Trying to appear inconspicuous, I turned at an angle while I continued singing so I could glance at the whiskey-breathed intruder. A young man, perhaps age twenty-five, maybe younger, sat alone in the pew, a drunken smile plastered across his unshaven face. His hair was bushy and uncombed, his clothing unbefitting a reverent church service. I did not recognize the fellow and later would learn that nobody else knew him either, which is odd in Georgetown, a friendly place where everyone seems to know everybody else, including their family trees.

I immediately realized that the man was confused, and not just with the Christmas Eve service, which for a first-time visitor can be somewhat perplexing. He was disoriented, in general. He stumbled aimlessly through the hymnal and a prayer book like a child leafing through coloring books at the doctor's office. He was obviously intoxicated and his behavior made me uncomfortable. Judging by the numerous nervous stares in the young man's direction, some subtle and some not so subtle, others shared my opinion.

A good-natured parishioner named Bob left his family and his regularly appointed pew and joined the fellow, shaking his hand and introducing himself with a warm smile. Bob helped the man throughout the remainder of the hymn sing, assisting the delighted guy with locating the proper songs and directing him with basic liturgical functions, such as when to stand, sit and kneel. With each song, the drunken stranger sang zealously louder and genuinely off key, although I suspect he felt he was performing as well as Pavarotti. I found his butchering of the traditional holiday carols both disturbing and amusing at the same time. Though he couldn't sing a lick, he certainly was having fun.

The hymn sing-a-long ended and the service began with "O Come, All Ye Faithful," as a procession of priests in robes and acolytes bearing torches entered from the back of the church. Someone in the procession waved a canister of incense, preparing the sanctuary for worship and God's presence, but it made my eyes water and I sneezed. The service continued with prayer and Bible readings about the birth of the Savior, the infant Jesus. Good Samaritan Bob continued to befriend the man, who grinned with delight, and I, my heart softening, traded smiles with him.

Why was I angry that he came here tonight? I thought. *This is God's house, not mine, and all are welcomed in the house of the Lord.*

I wondered whether the young man was lonely or depressed on this holiday eve, and had first sought the comfort of liquor, drowning unknown sorrows, and had somehow journeyed by our church. Perhaps he'd heard the festive Christmas music outside the ancient brick walls. Maybe he'd seen the church aglow through the windows, holly wreaths hanging from the huge oaken doors, like one of those wonderful Thomas Kinkade landscape portraits, so inviting. Perhaps something deep within his heart had prompted him to go inside. Maybe he simply needed to be in the warm company of other human beings. I wondered who he was and where he'd come from. Did he have a family? Was he married? Did he have children?

The priest moved to the pulpit to begin his Christmas homily. He had preached for only a few minutes when he abruptly stopped his sermon. I initially thought that he'd lost his place or was pausing for oratorical effect. But then I noticed him looking upon the congregation with a concerned frown rippling across his forehead. A low, curious murmur spread throughout the congregation. Everyone, including myself, looked to where the priest was gazing. About four pews back from the front, on the left side, Bill, an elderly man who faithfully attended every Sunday, had slumped over. Several members of the congregation had moved to his aid, thinking he had merely passed out. The situation, however, was far graver.

The service came to a complete halt as one parishioner sprinted to call 911. Several people laid Bill on his back in the pew and attempted to revive him. Although a medical doctor and several nurses were on hand that evening, the situation did not appear good. Bill was unconscious; he had stopped breathing, and his pulse was weak. Even from across the center aisle in dim lighting, I could see his flesh turning gray.

Stunned, most of us just sat or stood in our pews, paralyzed with fear and disbelief. A beloved man of our church community was dying before our eyes, and suddenly it no longer felt like Christmas Eve. I felt helpless, lost. Then a voice spoke out.

"Why don't we all get down on our knees and pray for the old guy," the voice bellowed from behind me. It was our visitor, his voice slurred but strong. "Maybe God can help him."

His words were like a slap in the face. Many of us snapped out of our panicked stupor and silently knelt in agreement with the man's suggestion. As several people continued to tend to Bill, the rest of the congregation prayed in honest, pleading whispers. I prayed harder and more sincerely than I ever had, my eyes tightly shut.

Moments later, I heard a commotion to my left. I opened my eyes just as I whispered "Amen" and was shocked to see Bill sitting up, his eyes open, the paleness in his face rapidly disappearing. Happy sobs could be heard throughout the church; our prayers had been gloriously answered! Despite numerous inquiries, Bill assured us that he was fine. When the paramedics arrived, racing down the center aisle with their equipment and stretcher, he refused to go to the hospital, insisting on staying for the conclusion of the Christmas Eve Mass. And after everything settled down, the service was, in fact, finished without further incident.

After the closing benediction and song—a rousing "Joy to the World"—I turned to shake the young man's hand, but he was gone. He had apparently left during the Eucharist as the congregation filed pew by pew for the bread and wine, the body and blood of our Savior.

I later discovered that no one else had seen the man leave either. It was as if he'd appeared out of nowhere and then simply vanished into

thin air. No one knew his identity or anything about him. He was no one's relative, or neighbor, or co-worker. No one knew or ever saw again the man who visited us that Christmas Eve, when a whole church witnessed a miracle. A dying man was revived, saved from death, by prayer initiated by a stranger, a person like you or me, or perhaps the guy we pass every day in the street and pay no attention to, an unlikely angel who prays for our health and happiness, for peace and good will to all.

OUT OF THE NIGHT

JACK HARING

Christmas Day 1944

Dear Mom,

    This is a very different Christmas Day than I have ever spent in my life. Right now I'm living in the hayloft of a farmer's barn, and I'm very glad to be here rather than out in a foxhole somewhere. . . .

The Battle of the Bulge. The final desperate attempt of the Germans to break through Allied lines in Belgium and dash to Antwerp and the sea. For six days our Eighty-fourth Infantry Division had been diverted from the Ninth Army in the north to the beleaguered First Army area in the Ardennes forest. The fiercest fighting of the war, and I, a nineteen-year-old private, was in the middle of it.

My letter home to Pennsylvania was written on a Christmas morning that was sunny and quiet—deceptively quiet. "The barn I slept in last night," I wrote, "made me think of the place where Jesus came into the world." Then I began reminiscing to Mom about the good Christmases we'd had as I was growing up—always starting with the traditional dawn service at St. John's Lutheran in Boyertown. Church had always been an

important part of my life. I'd started college thinking I might go into the ministry.

The letter home was upbeat all the way. I didn't mention anything about the things that had been troubling me. How I had become disillusioned with organized religion because I saw so few Christians either at home or in the combat zone—certainly not Christians trying to live the way Jesus had taught. Or how the weather had been so miserable and the fighting so blazing that I feared I'd never live to see Pennsylvania again.

The last straw was being sent to these snow-covered hills and woods where we might be attacked at any moment from out there, somewhere. I was beginning to think that God had forsaken me.

Still, even though we'd spent the last five days floundering around trying to stop the Germans, even though our supply trucks had been captured, at least we'd had a barn for shelter on Christmas Eve, and our cooks were promising us a hot meal for Christmas Day.

"Let's go, men," Sergeant Presto, our squad leader, shouted. "Collect your gear and fall out. We're going on a mission."

I groaned. We all groaned. There went our first hot meal in a week!

We drove for about ten miles and then the trucks dropped us and sped away. It was dusk. Troops were strung out all along a dirt road that circled through some hills. When Presto came back from a meeting with the platoon leader, he gathered the ten of us—we were one man short in the squad—around him.

"Okay, men, here's what we're going to do. This won't take long and we're going to travel light. Leave your packs and entrenching tools here." He made it sound so simple. Intelligence had said that some German infantry were dug into a nearby hill and were causing havoc by shooting

down on the roads in the area. Our battalion's job was to go up and flush them out.

Single file on each side of the winding road, we moved up the hill. We moved quietly, warily. At the top, we were surprised to find, not Germans, but an abandoned chateau in the middle of a clearing. Our squad went into the building. We found a billiard table and the tension broke as we played an imaginary game of pool using our rifles as cues.

Then Presto came stalking in. The Germans, he said, were in the woods beyond the clearing. Our orders were to chase them out into the waiting arms of another battalion positioned at the other end of the woods.

"There'll be three companies in this deal," Presto said. "Two of us will stretch out along the edge of the forest while the other hangs back in reserve. Now, as soon as we push into the woods, everybody fires, got it?"

We spread out, walked through the darkness to the forest's edge, then, at a signal, we burst in, opening up with everything we had. We kept up a brisk pace, keeping contact with our buddies along the moving line, walking and firing for about a mile. But the forest was empty. There was no movement. . . .

The trees in front of us exploded. Suddenly, the night went bright with every kind of firing I'd ever seen or heard of—rifles, rifle-launched grenades, mortars, machine guns, tracers over our heads, bullets at our thighs. But worst of all, Tiger tanks. At least six of them, opening up point-blank with 88-millimeter cannons. Their projectiles whined and crashed all up and down our line.

Our intelligence was wrong, I thought angrily, as I flung myself down on my stomach. *They told us there were no tanks up here. Now we're really in for it.*

Within seconds men were screaming in pain all around me. I saw a tree

with a big trunk and made a sudden lunge to get behind it, but I wasn't quick enough. Something tore into my thigh. There was hot, searing pain.

We were completely pinned down. The Tiger tanks kept scanning their turrets and firing on every yard of our line. The German ground troops sent their small-arms fire into anything that moved.

The minutes went by. Five. Ten. Fifteen. Then came a lull in the barrage. I called over to my best buddy, Kane. We called him "Killer." He was the gentlest guy in our platoon, but we'd nicknamed him that after the popular comic strip character, "Killer Kane."

"Are you hurt, Killer?"

"Naw. But I think everybody else over here is. Presto's hit bad."

I called to Cruz on my right. He was our squad's B.A.R. man. There was no answer. Then I barely heard him whispering, "I'm hurt. Real bad. Floyd's dead. Corporal John's hit bad."

Well, I thought, *if Presto's out and the Corporal, too, we don't have a leader.*

The pounding started again, this time with flares so they could spot us better. We did some firing back and then the action subsided into another lull.

Down along the rear of our line came a figure, crawling. It was our platoon runner. "Captain says we're getting nowhere," he whispered to Killer and me. "We're pulling back in five minutes. Move out when you hear our covering fire."

I crawled over to Killer. "We've got to get our guys out of here," I said. "You go up your side and I'll go down mine, and we'll drag as many as possible to that big tree back there."

"How're we going to get them out of here, though?"

"I don't know," I said. "But we can't leave them lying here."

We were trapped. I lay there on the cold ground feeling helpless, that forsaken feeling again. Where was the God that I had prayed to during all those years of church and Sunday school back home in Pennsylvania? "And whatsoever ye shall ask in my name, that will I do," the Bible had said to me clearly (John 14:13). Was it necessary, when I needed help so badly, to ask?

"O Lord," I mumbled, "help us. We're trying to get our wounded buddies out of here. Show us the way."

I had no sooner started dragging Corporal John toward our meeting tree when the firing started up in the center of our line. *There's the signal for pulling back*, I thought frantically, *but we can't do it. The Germans will sweep in on us; they'll mop us up before we can pull back.*

Just as I got to the tree, I saw that Killer had brought back three wounded squad members. So we had six wounded to get back. I closed my eyes and in desperation said: "In Your name, Lord, help us."

I opened my eyes. In the black of night, moving mysteriously among the shattered trees, a giant hulk came toward us. *The Germans*, my heart thumped, *they've broken out of the brush. They're bearing down on us.* No, it was something else, something unbelievable. It now came into full view and stopped beside our tree.

A horse.

A big, docile, shaggy chestnut, standing there without a harness, as though awaiting our bidding.

Killer and I looked at each other in disbelief. We didn't question then where the horse came from, or how, or why; we just got to work. Moving swiftly, we draped Cruz and the Corporal on the chestnut's broad back, then Mike and Presto. Then, with Killer carrying one of our buddies and me carrying the other, we led the horse out of the woods. At the clearing the horse trotted on ahead of us, straight to the chateau, and by the time Killer and I got there, the four wounded were already on medical stretchers. The two men we carried in were cared for; the medics took a quick look at my shrapnel wound; and then, as fast as we could, Killer and I went to find the horse. We wanted to pat him, give him some sugar, anything to make him sense our gratitude.

But he wasn't there. We looked everywhere, asked everyone we saw, but no one could tell us anything about him. He had simply vanished—gone from us as mysteriously as he had come.

The next morning at the aid station the shrapnel was removed from my leg, and at noon Killer and I lined up for our belated Christmas dinner. The day before, 190 men in our company would have answered the chow call; today there were thirty-five of us. At least the wounded men in our squad had survived, however, though some were never to see action again.

Killer and I looked at the turkey and sweet potatoes in our mess kits. Hot and savory and long-awaited as this food was, we had no appetite. We were still too full of our emotions: the sorrow for the buddies we had lost; the shock of our own survival; the strange, deeply affecting arrival and departure of the horse. We could not get the horse out of our minds then, nor have I since, for that noble creature did more than just save our lives—he reaffirmed my faith. I have always believed that on that Christmas night thirty-three years ago, God sent that horse to reassure a doubting soldier of His presence, even as He had sent His Son for that purpose on a Christmas night twenty centuries ago.

MAMA'S PAPER ROSES

MITZI CARBAUGH

While I was growing up in Mobile, Alabama, my father was often out of work, and it was up to Mama to find a way to make ends meet. That wasn't easy with five children to feed and clothe. Yet somehow, miraculously, she always found a way. The Christmas I was six, my two older sisters had moved out, so it was just me, my big brother Junior, and my baby sister at home. What money we had went for groceries, maybe a few simple presents, but we couldn't possibly afford a tree. Daddy took us all out into the woods, where we picked a scruffy pine to drag inside. But what about decorations? "I think I can find some," Mama said softly. She opened a cabinet that held a collection of gold foil rings pulled off cigars. "I knew these would come in handy someday," she said as she showed us how perfectly the rings fit over the tips of the tree branches. She made a garland out of colorful rags, tying the pieces together into a chain. Our tree was being transformed before our very eyes.

"A tree fit for a king," Daddy declared when we were finished.

Then Mama explained how Jesus was a king, even though his parents didn't have a lot of money. "But that's impossible, Mama. Everybody knows a poor child can't be king."

"With God, Mitzi, all things are possible," Mama said. "That's what we remember each year when we celebrate Jesus' birthday." I looked at our tree and imagined the presents with our names on them that would be waiting for us kids Christmas morning. Maybe nothing fancy like a king would have, but wonderful presents just the same.

We found Mama stirring a pot at the stove the next morning. "What's that, Mama?" I asked. "Breakfast?"

Mama shook her head. "It's hot wax," she said. "Now stand back." Junior and I watched Mama take the pot off the burner. On the table were brightly colored crepe paper, some old hangers and a pair of sturdy scissors. "Watch," Mama said. She plucked a bright pink sheet of crepe paper from the pile and cut out a funny-shaped piece that looked like a heart with a tail. Then she untwisted the hanger and straightened it out. She took the scissors to that too, squeezing her hands hard to cut the wire in half. "This will be a stem," she said. Mama's fingers were red and pinched, but she went right to work, wrapping the tail part of the crepe paper around the stem. After she had four pieces wrapped around the wire, Mama curled the heart-shaped ends out at the top like petals.

Mama proudly held up what she had made. "A rose!" I gasped as she held the stem and dipped the paper flower in the hot wax so the bright rose shone like real petals sparkling with early-morning dew.

"Can we help you make another, Mama?" Junior asked.

"Of course," said Mama. "How could I do it without your help?" All morning the three of us sat at the table making paper roses: pink, white, red and my favorite, bright yellow. Well, it was Mama who really did the work, but Junior and I picked out the colors and made Mama laugh while she wrapped and curled and dipped. By the middle of the afternoon bunches of roses lay across the table.

"It looks like a garden in the middle of winter!" I exclaimed. "What are we going to do with them all?"

Mama went to the closet and took out our coats. "I have a very special job for you," she said, brushing our hair and making sure our hands were clean. Junior and I nodded solemnly. We could handle a special job! Mama explained how we were to go to people's houses and ask if they would like to buy some roses. "Sixty cents for a dozen, thirty cents for six," Mama said. Junior and I repeated the price three times to be sure we got it right. "Now you two stick together, and don't go inside anywhere," Mama instructed as she buttoned up my coat. Her fingers were sore from cutting all of the wire to make the stems, and there were blisters on her hands from where the wax had splattered on her. "And don't take anything besides the money."

"Yes, Mama," we promised as we stepped out the door. The wind was strong, but Junior and I wrapped our arms around the roses to keep them safe. We visited plenty of houses that day, and it seemed like everyone wanted Mama's paper roses for Christmas.

"Just one more bunch, and we'll have sold them all," I told Junior proudly as we rang the doorbell at a large house with a big wreath on the door. A woman in an apron answered.

"What beautiful roses!" she exclaimed. "Come inside and keep warm while I get my purse. Would you children like some cookies?"

"No, thank you, ma'am," Junior said politely, just as Mama always taught us. "We'll wait out here." But when the lady was gone we peeked inside the open door. "Mitzi, look!" Junior whispered. In the corner of the hall was a tremendous fir tree covered in gold and silver balls and twinkling lights, with a glowing star on top. I'd never seen such a tree in all my life!

"It's much fancier than ours," I observed.

Junior nodded. "But I like ours better."

I took one more look at the tree. "Yeah," I agreed. "Our tree is special. It's a tree fit for a king."

On the way home Junior and I discussed what kind of presents the people in that house might be getting. "I'll bet the kids get tons of presents," Junior sighed. "Maybe even roller skates!" Roller skates! That was just about the biggest present we could imagine.

Mama was waiting with hot cocoa and blankets when we got home. "We were real careful with the money," Junior told her as we pulled handfuls of nickels and dimes out of our pockets.

"You did a good job," Mama said, helping us off with our coats. "I don't know what I would do without you two."

The next week Mama made lots more roses, and Junior and I sold every single one. "I'm going to miss going door to door," I said as Junior and I went to bed on Christmas Eve. "But we'll definitely have enough money for groceries now."

Bright and early the next morning I bounded out of bed and down to our tree. Sure enough, Santa had left a present for each of us kids, even the baby. There were two wrapped packages just the same size, one with my name on it and one with Junior's. "What do you suppose those are?" Daddy asked. We carried the boxes to the middle of the room. They were surprisingly heavy. I shook mine a little and heard a thump from inside. What could it be? Junior and I tore off the wrapping paper.

I gasped. "Mama! Roller skates!"

Junior pulled his skates out of the box, turning them over in his hands like he was making sure they were real. "Let's see them," said Mama. We rushed to her side and held up the silver skates so Mama could spin the wheels with her hands, still cracked and blistered from making those paper roses.

"Santa brought us roller skates!" I said. I could still hardly believe it was true. But hadn't Mama said at Christmastime anything was possible?

"Of course he did," Mama said, sweeping us into a big hug. "Because you're such a good boy and girl!"

It was years before I questioned where those roller skates really came from, or wondered just what Mama did with the money she worked so hard for that Christmas. Looking back, though, I think that was just the way Mama wanted it. On that magic morning, I knew without a doubt that all things are possible—that roses can bloom in wintertime and a poor child can be King.

"TELLING ME ALWAYS TO BELIEVE"

CANDY CHAND

Cliff was a special man, a priceless gift. His tender heart, his deep spiritual faith, were qualities that permeated his presence. An uncle by marriage, Cliff came into Kathy's life with a depth that stemmed from many hours in prayer, many hours in the presence of God.

In 1965, Cliff lost his wife on a lonely, gray December day. He rarely spoke of her, but his countenance revealed a love beyond measure. His home was filled with memories, a legacy of her life on earth. Cliff hoped to see his wife once more, in a place without distance, in a time without end.

For many, Christmas brings sorrow: reminders from years gone by, of love long departed. Each December, Kathy would visit her uncle, if only to warm his home with laughter, to drink a cup of soothing cocoa and fill his day with cheer.

Many Christmases came and went, each season flowing endlessly into the next. And in 1986, as we someday all must do, her dear uncle came to his final day on earth. Christmas, for Kathy, would never be the same.

Weeks after Cliff's death, a small wooden box was discovered among

his belongings. Inside were beautiful poems, revealing her uncle's deepest thoughts, secrets and emotions. He had written them for years, some to his wife, some to his God, some to the family who would surely find them one day.

A particular poem touched Kathy's heart. Next to the beautifully penned words was an inscription. It read, "This is a true experience. It happened Christmas Day 1973."

Then a Bible verse followed: "Behold, I send an angel before thee, to keep thee in the way, and bring thee into the place which I have prepared" (Exodus 23:20).

Kathy began to read:

> *An angel came into my dreams,*
> *So lovely and so fair,*
> *Her eyes were blue as blue can be,*
> *Cascading gold her shining hair.*

> *From whence she came I never knew*
> *Nor where she went when taking leave*
> *Tarrying but a little while,*
> *Telling me always to believe.*

> *Ever and anon she returned again*
> *In the stillness of the night,*
> *And the beauty of her presence,*
> *Was a softly glowing light.*

I longed to find this little girl,
And make a sacred vow,
For I could see the grace of God,
Resting on her brow.

Then, lo, one cheerless Christmas Day,
She came to my lonely door,
With a kitten cradled in her arms,
A gift of love forevermore.

So my dreams weren't only dreams,
But a vision of things to come,
For she came and stayed, then went away,
And never said where she was from.

Oh to see her once again,
my forlorn soul I'd give
To touch her golden halo,
And once again, to live.

Kathy's heart melted. Her uncle had once received an angelic visitor on Christmas day! As she continued to read, tears began to fall. Kathy was comforted with the assurance that her dear uncle was now in the presence of God, embraced in the arms of his beloved wife. He'd been escorted, hand in hand, by a golden-haired angel—an angel who returned to take him home, where, once again, he lives.

CHAPTER NINE

ANSWERING PRAYER

O holy Child of Bethlehem,
Descend to us, we pray.

L ord, hear our prayer." It is a phrase for any season. But prayers asked—and answered—at Christmastime seem especially meaningful to children and adults alike. *Yes, the holy Child of Bethlehem is here, still here, among us.*

For the prayers whose stories appear in this section, God, as is often the case, chose to respond creatively. He sent His angels, heavenly and earthly, to answer their Christmas prayers dramatically —for gifts, for comfort, for strength and endurance. In the last story, Joyce Reagin wraps her own prayer of relinquishment— and her obedience to an inner voice—around another person's request for money, which results in a generous act of charity.

This and other stories give new meaning to a very personal request: "Lord, hear my Christmas prayer. Be with us and meet our needs." They also remind us that sometimes we are the answer to someone else's prayer.

—E.B.

MYSTERY TRAIN

GERALDINE JOAN MORRIS

Eight was old enough to find out the truth about Santa Claus. Usually my eight brothers and sisters and I got apples or nuts for Christmas, but I knew kids from wealthy families got toys. The real Santa wouldn't care about money. "Please take me to see him at the department store," I asked my mother.

My heart fluttered as I waited in line. *He sure looks like Santa*, I thought. Finally I was next. A lady put her hand out to stop me.

"A quarter," she said to my mother. "Your daughter can pick a present."

Mama blushed. She didn't have a quarter. "She just wants to talk to him," Mama said softly.

"I'm sorry," said the woman. I had my answer: Santa wasn't real.

I told my brother Jimmy to stop asking Santa for that electric train. "I'll pray for one instead," Jimmy said. I prayed too. We all did. But I was worried. What if God was a fake too?

On Christmas morning a beautiful electric train waited under the tree. All us kids cheered. "I met the lady who just moved into the yellow house up the block," Mama explained to me in secret. "She asked if we'd like her grown son's train."

Mama sent my oldest brothers to the yellow house with Christmas cookies. A man answered. He knew nothing about a lady or an electric train. I guess God was the "real" Santa all along.

A DOG NAMED BANDIT

RONALD "SCOTTY" BOURNE

For the past ten years I have been placing a little figure of a dog next to the infant Jesus in my Nativity set at Christmas. Some people raise their eyebrows, but when they hear my story, they feel differently. For it represents a real dog, named Bandit. Whether he belongs there, you judge for yourself.

I got Bandit in 1967 when I was working as an animal trainer for Walt Disney Productions. We were filming *Three Without Fear*, a TV movie about three children and a dog trekking across a desert. We needed an animal that looked like a starved Mexican street dog.

At an animal shelter in Glendale, I found a part German shepherd. His ribs protruding through his mangy black-and-gray fur, he fit the part. Bandit was what local children had called him for stealing food.

Bandit turned out to be a natural actor. He took direction well and was always ready to play. Sometimes the play got out of hand. When we were filming near Scammon's Lagoon in Mexico, someone threw a stick into the ocean for him to retrieve. A strong undertow carried him along the shore. As he struggled to keep his nose above water, I raced along the high sandbank, trying to reach him before he was carried out to sea. At the last second, I managed to grab his collar and pull him to safety.

Another time, in Arizona, a little raccoonlike animal called a coatimundi, which was appearing in a scene with him, bit Bandit's leg. The animal's razor-sharp teeth severed an artery, and two crew members and I made a mad dash by car sixty miles across the desert to a Tucson veterinarian. As I held Bandit in my arms, I realized how much my friend meant to me. Thank God, a fine vet helped pull Bandit through. I decided then it was time he retired from the movies.

For a while Bandit lived with my sister's family in Simi Valley. He thrived on domestic life and became a neighborhood hero: As his movies appeared on television, there was a constant demand for him to "speak," "shake hands" and pose for pictures. Bandit loved the attention and had infinite patience.

Moreover, he had an almost human understanding of people's needs. For example, one of my sister's boys was born with splayed feet. The doctor prescribed braces and told her not to expect the child to walk at the normal time. But one day, to everyone's surprise, Bandit was seen walking very slowly across the yard with the baby toddling behind, hanging on to the dog's bushy tail!

Then came a time when everything in my life fell apart. After a broken romance, I was at my lowest ebb. Bandit and I got back together again, and during long reflective walks on the beach, he was my only companion. Though now graying at his muzzle, he still wanted me to throw a ball and play with him. This was my therapy, for Bandit coaxed me out of my melancholy solitude.

As my outlook improved I deepened my relationship with the Lord.

This led me into many new areas, one of which was a juvenile prison ministry. Bandit accompanied me on my visits to the teenage boys; they loved to hear his story, especially about my finding him in "prison."

But by 1979 Bandit was old and painfully stiff; I sensed it would be his last Christmas, and I asked the Lord to help me make it especially significant, not only because of Bandit, but because of my new life with God.

By mid-December I was afraid Bandit would not even make it to Christmas. One day while praying over him, I envisioned myself going to the stable at Bethlehem. Carrying my old friend in my arms, I presented him to the infant Jesus. I explained to Jesus that my gift was the only treasure I had left. Slowly, I placed Bandit beside the baby Jesus, then turned and walked away.

The picture I had while praying became a reality on Christmas Eve. Bandit lay on the lawn, unable to stand. His brown eyes, glazed with pain, looked up at me imploringly. In anguish I called the animal shelter, and I placed Bandit in my car for the last time. The man at the shelter took him gently, and I stood waiting outside until he brought me Bandit's collar; he put his hand on my shoulder and told me it was all over.

All the way home I begged, "Lord, I know he was just a dog, but he meant the world to me and I loved him. Please let me know if he is with You."

I was still grieving the next morning as I arrived at the detention camp to conduct a Christmas communion service. I really didn't feel like being there. The boys were at a low point too, for they had nothing to give their families, who would be visiting later in the day. Our service was held in a small television room, the only decoration being a simple Nativity set on the table that served as an altar.

As I talked to the boys about the spirit of giving, I said, "People place too much emphasis on expensive gifts. The greatest gift you can give is what you seem to place the least value on. While we're taking communion, I suggest each of you offer Jesus the one precious gift that no one else can give: yourself."

When it was over, as the boys started filing out the door, I happened to look down at the manger scene. I stared transfixed. Standing beside the crib of the baby Jesus was a little statue of a dog. A dog that looked like Bandit—in the exact spot where I had placed him in my prayer.

With a tight throat I asked, "Who—where did the dog come from?" The boys all shook their heads.

No one at the center had any idea who put the small figure of a dog there or where it came from. So I gently put the figure in my pocket, looked up and silently thanked God for answering my prayer.

And that's why I have a little dog next to the baby Jesus in my crèche.

FIVE LOST MINUTES

JOAN WESTER ANDERSON

Diane Barnard (not her real name) doesn't believe in coincidences. She remembers a very special Christmas Eve when she asked for help—and received it.

Snow had been falling all that day in Rittman, Ohio. The white covering was now almost a foot deep, and although it looked beautiful, driving was virtually impossible. For twenty-three-year-old Diane, however, walking was just fine. Even though she lived more than a mile from church, she was so happy to be going to midnight services that she didn't mind the trek—or the fact that she would have to travel alone because her husband would stay home and care for their toddler. Christmas was just the very best time of year!

At about eleven o'clock, Diane said good-bye to her husband and set out. Although the drifts were quite high in places, the journey was downhill, and she got to the church with time to spare.

The festive and beautiful ceremony ended just before one in the morning. Diane hadn't encountered neighbors or friends who might have given her a ride home, so she started her hike. But getting *up* the hill was a far different matter from going down. Each step now seemed deeper and more difficult than the one preceding it, and her path was both dark and deserted, with no homes nearby. Diane's breathing came in small gasps as she plodded onward. Oh, she was tired! And as she passed a barren wooded area, she became even more alarmed.

"My feet were getting heavier with each step, and I started to realize that I was in trouble," she says. "There was a distinct possibility that I actually wasn't going to make it home—I was just too cold and weary. Would my husband wake up and realize I was missing? Would anyone find me here, or would I fall and freeze?" Her joyous excursion was rapidly turning into a nightmare.

Diane looked at her watch: one-fifteen. There was still a long way to go to reach warmth and safety, and her strength was virtually at an end. She gazed at the star-studded Christmas heavens. "Oh, God, I'm so afraid," she blurted. "Help me to get home!"

Suddenly Diane heard beautiful music—and felt herself floating on top of the snow, as if she were in a dream. What was happening? Was she freezing? Is this how it felt to die?

No. She was, oddly, in front of her house. But how could this be? Diane blinked, looked at the familiar landmarks, then at her watch again. It was one-twenty. And yet she had no memory of moving since she had prayed. Certainly five minutes had not elapsed. Nor would she, in her exhausted condition, have been able to scale the steep hill looming in front of her. She had been ready to lie down in the snow and give up the struggle.

And yet she was safely home and feeling . . . exultant.

The young mother entered her quiet house and, still wearing her coat and boots, sat in a chair and looked at the winking Christmas lights. "I

don't remember how long I sat," she says now, "but I knew something strange had happened to me, and I was afraid even to admit it to myself.

"But I've come up with no other explanation in all the years since then. I think it was an angel, commanded by God to carry me safely to my front door." A member of the heavenly host, perhaps, leaving his duties on a Bethlehem hillside to touch a young woman in Ohio.

A CUPBOARD
OF MY VERY OWN

LAURA LEE C. ADKINS

When I was growing up in the 1950s in Long Beach, California, times were tough for my family. It was just my sister Donna, my mother and me, and we were pretty poor. Mom—who had only an eighth-grade education—worked as a night nurse (back then a person didn't need the training required today), but the job didn't pay all that much.

"I don't know how I'm gonna feed you kids," she worried. Times were tough, and sometimes food was scarce. But we made do. In fact, we thought chicken necks or hamburger was an elegant meal. And once in a while Mother would ask the butcher for a beef bone that she would simmer for soups or stews. When Mother was through making our meal she'd give the dog the bone. We were happy and so was the dog.

The happiest times, though, were the holidays, especially Christmas. Each year Donna and I unwrapped the ornaments and set up the Nativity scene, waiting for the moment when we'd start decorating the tree! Mother was always able to make a deal with the man who owned the tree lot for one of the less desirable trees. The branches on those trees were always spaced widely apart, leaving gaping holes. Mom would prop the tree up in a corner with the barest patch facing the wall. The rest of the gaps were disguised by ornaments or tinsel.

There never were many presents under the tree, but that didn't stop Donna and me from dreaming about all the things we might get, like a baby doll, a wagon or a scooter. We didn't ever get those kinds of gifts. Usually the Salvation Army delivered a basket to our house before Christmas. Inside was enough food for a holiday dinner, and occasionally some secondhand clothes.

The Christmas of 1956, though, was different. I remember my mother sitting us down, bubbling with excitement as she announced that three days before Christmas our neighbor's lodge would be sponsoring a party for needy children, and we had been invited. I was five and Donna was eight; neither of us was quite sure what "needy" children were, but we were children who needed things, so that must've meant us. Then Mother said Santa Claus would be at the party to give out presents! I lay awake in bed at night thinking about it. *Jesus,* I'd pray, *please let Santa give me the present I want.* I knew I shouldn't ask for a lot, but maybe just this once it was okay to pray for a special gift. I thought long and hard about what it was I wanted most of all.

After a long wait, December 22 rolled around. Mother washed and ironed the clothes my sister and I would wear, then bathed us, dressed us and fixed our hair so we'd look our best for the party. Our neighbors drove us in their car. As soon as we walked through the lodge door, I was overwhelmed. There were rows and rows of tables stacked with more food than I'd seen in my entire life. There were adults laughing and talking, and children staring wide-eyed at the gigantic tree right in the middle of the room. No wonder, because underneath that tree were piled hundreds of presents—dolls, fire trucks, balls, all sorts of things.

"Okay, kids," someone announced. "Santa's coming. Get in line to sit on his lap. You can ask for anything you want as long as you see it over there under the tree."

Oh well, I thought, deflated. The toys I saw were enough to make any boy or girl swoon, but what I wanted, what I'd spent so long thinking about, what I'd finally ended up asking God for, wasn't under the tree. And though I was only five, I'd already learned how to make do with what was at hand. So I resolved to change my mind and ask Santa for something else.

When my turn came, Santa asked, "What would a pretty girl like you want?" When I heard that question, my resolve melted. I just couldn't keep my secret to myself. I blurted out, "I want a kitchen cupboard with my very own food in it!"

"A cupboard?" Santa asked. "You mean a little play kitchen?"

"No, Santa," I said. "My own real cupboard. With real food."

"Ah, well," he mumbled. "What a wonderful gift that would be." He seemed unsure of what to say next. "I didn't have enough room on my sleigh for a present that large," he told me finally.

I felt bad for letting out my secret. "One of those stuffed animals under the tree would be nice," I said.

"Good choice!" Santa told me. On the ride home I looked at the stuffed bear I'd picked. For the first time I knew not all requests made to Santa, or to God, could be granted. All of a sudden I felt greedy. Who was I to have wanted such a thing in the first place? It had been asking too much. Besides, it was Baby Jesus' birthday we were celebrating, not mine.

My shame was short-lived; by the time Christmas morning came I'd almost forgotten about it. I was still excited about Christmas, and my sister and I rushed to our own tree as soon as we woke, hoping there might be something under it for us. And there was! Four beautifully wrapped presents! We ripped the bows and paper off the first two, finding a pair of socks for each of us. The other presents were brand-new coloring books. *I guess Santa didn't give up on me after all*, I thought.

I was scribbling away in my new coloring book when a knock came at the back door. My mother got up to answer it. When I heard her talking, I turned to look and saw her motion for me to come to the door. Standing there was our neighbor from the lodge, and right next to him was Santa, holding something. "I think that's for you, dear," Mother said.

"Sorry I couldn't deliver this last night," Santa said. "Like I told you, it wouldn't fit on my sleigh."

My eyes grew wide as I realized what it was. "My very own cupboard!" I shouted.

It was painted white, with hinged doors. And when I opened those doors, I couldn't believe what was inside. The shelves were packed with food. I was speechless. I hugged Santa, and when I could finally talk I said thank you over and over.

"Your very own cupboard," he said. "You and your mother can cook your family many wonderful meals with that food."

"Oh, we will. I promise," I replied.

I've seen a lot of Christmases since then, and I've gotten many gifts. But none has ever been quite like that cupboard of my very own from Santa. Sometimes God puts people in our lives who give us what we want most when we need it most. And every Christmas since, I've tried to be one of those people for someone else, a kind of Santa, passing the gift on.

A PROMISE, A PRAYER,
A QUIET VOICE

JOYCE REAGIN

December 7, 1980, was one of those pre-Christmas Sundays that was meant to be full of candles, carols and great expectations. After church my husband Earl and I planned to take our young sons for a holiday portrait. Then a ride to look at neighborhood Christmas decorations would put us in the mood for a family shopping trip and other errands punctuated by whisperings and giggled secrets.

We missed church. On top of that, Grant, age seven, and his brother, Britt, age four, did not want to get dressed up for a photograph sitting. They whined all the way to the studio, where the photographer could find no evidence of our appointment and could not work us in. The ensuing Christmas ride was more dismal yet. But the capper was yet to come. I opened my purse only to discover that the rest of our Christmas money was gone. I had lost about a hundred dollars in cash.

A hundred dollars might not be a lot of money to lose, but it was important to us because we had, for the first time in our marriage, managed to adhere strictly to a Christmas budget.

Perhaps I'd been a little too proud! Earlier that very afternoon, while riding around in the car, I'd drawn the gray bank envelope from my purse and shown the bills inside to Earl and the boys. "Aren't you proud of me? Mom's actually managed to budget the Christmas money!"

That was the last time any of us saw the envelope. Evidently I had not put it back into my purse but had laid it on the seat. During the course of our afternoon stops, it must have fallen unnoticed from the car.

"It's Christmas," I explained to Earl. "People steal money this time of year. I'm sure someone has found it. An envelope full of cash, with no name, no identification! Who could blame someone for keeping it?"

All evening I stewed. As we prepared for bed, Earl put his arms around me and kissed me. "Please, darling, stop thinking about the money. Tomorrow we'll retrace our steps. Who knows? Maybe someone has turned it in." We prayed together that I'd have peace about the money and that we'd find it again if it was God's will.

It didn't help a bit. I tossed and turned all night.

The next morning it was difficult to concentrate on teaching my classes at school. I kept thinking about the lost money, about my carelessness, my stupidity, about the gifts we still had to buy.

And then it came to me—the two hundred dollars.

In the fall, Earl and I had set aside two hundred dollars in a savings account because we felt God wanted us to give that money to an individual or family in need. We'd been asking God to direct our path.

Then a stronger, inner voice reminded me: that was not our money, that was God's money. As tempting as it was, that money was not for me to spend.

After work, Earl and I retraced our path. No one had turned in money at the filling station where we'd bought gas. Nor had anything been found at the cemetery, where we'd taken flowers to my grandmother's grave. The driveway at our own home was empty, of course.

But a change was beginning to take place in me. At home that night, I went into the bedroom and knelt alone. "Dear God," I prayed, "I can't stand this worried feeling. Please help me to release this matter to You. I know that all of our money is Yours, including that hundred dollars. If it's Your will, please return the money to us. If it's not, I release that money, I give it freely to You and, through You, to whoever found it.

"And," I added, "I also release my carelessness on Sunday. If You can use even that for good, please go ahead. In Jesus' name, amen."

A peace stole over me. Not surprisingly, the house seemed brighter. The boys started laughing again, and we all joined in on snatches of carols.

The next day the sky was the brilliant blue that God saves for winter skies. I hummed as I headed for school, and taught my lessons without even thinking of the money.

Then, just before break time, I heard a still, small voice. *Go and call the places where you stopped on Sunday.*

But, God, I thought, *we went back to all those places yesterday.*

Go and call.

Obediently, excitedly, I hurried to the phone. First I called the gas station. "I may have lost some money there," I began.

"No," the lady clipped.

Next was the cemetery. I felt funny about making that call, but I dialed anyway. The manager answered.

Feeling foolish, I said, "Last Sunday I lost some money—"

He interrupted me. "How much?"

"Almost a hundred dollars. The money was stuffed into a gray bank envelope."

"How about ninety-six dollars?" he asked.

"You have it!" I exclaimed.

"Sure do. A gravedigger found it while he was picking up trash. He turned it in, said he thought it might be somebody's Christmas money."

After school I rushed to the cemetery office. The man who found it, Rubin Sales, was not there. Holding the dirt-smeared, tire-streaked envelope, I marveled that he had even bothered to look inside.

"Please tell him thank you," I said, leaving ten dollars for him.

I wasn't even out of the cemetery before that quiet voice spoke once more. *Rubin Sales is the one I want you to give the two hundred dollars to.* Excitedly I went to find Earl.

The very next day we went back to the cemetery to meet Rubin Sales. He was a middle-aged man, tall and muscular. But when we introduced ourselves, he looked at us almost shyly.

"Mr. Sales," I said, "thank you so much for finding and returning our money. Now we'd like to give some to you."

He firmly shook his head no without speaking.

"But, Mr. Sales—" I started.

"Thank you," he said, "but no. No reward. When I first saw that envelope, it just looked like trash. But something told me to look inside. Then something told me that was somebody's Christmas money." He paused. "I grew up poor. I know what it's like to hope and pray for something. And I didn't want any children's hopes not to come true."

"You don't understand," Earl answered. "This isn't a reward. This is

God's money. We've been keeping it until God told us what to do with it. And we believe He's told us this two hundred dollars is yours."

No one spoke for a moment. Earl's odd pronouncement hung in the chilly air.

"Exactly two hundred dollars?" Sales asked. His voice had a strange crack to it.

We nodded.

"I've been scrimping and saving to meet my bills," he said, "and last night when I sat down to pay them, there wasn't even near enough. As I worried what to do, a program about world hunger came on the television. When I saw the faces of those starving children, my own problems seemed so tiny. I wanted to help so badly, but all I could do was pray. I prayed for a way to pay my bills so I could send the money I had saved to help those little ones."

"And how much are your bills?" Earl asked, although we already knew the answer.

"Exactly two hundred dollars," he said.

"Merry Christmas, Mr. Sales," I said as we handed him the envelope.

CHAPTER TEN

HERALDING AND ESCORTING LIFE

Cast out our sin, and enter in,
Be born in us today.

C hristmas. At its core it is a celebration of birth. Not just any birth, but the birth of God-made-human. And yet this one particular birth prompts us to look at and reflect on anything and everything that brings new life: the birth of a calf delivers a Christmas message to Phyllis Tickle; a Christmastime spiritual birth comes to Earl Weirich and T. J. O'Bannan when mysterious strangers facilitate new life in Christ; someone pays the postage when Colleen Messina unwittingly mails *life* to her dad; and Sheila Hutcherson tells a different kind of escort-to-life story, placed here because of the truth in the line attributed to St. Francis of Assisi: "And it is in dying that we are born to eternal life."

Read on. Delight in the joy of birth, which was the angel's message: "For unto you is born this day . . . a Saviour, which is Christ the Lord" (Luke 2:11). *This* day allow Him to be born again, in you.

— E.B.

A COW, A CALF,
A CHRISTMAS MESSAGE

PHYLLIS TICKLE

Mother of seven children and wife of a physician,
Phyllis Tickle remembers the first winter after pursuing their dream
of moving out of the city, into the Tennessee countryside.

I t was 1977, the first winter since our coming to the farm, and the first day after Christmas. We had settled into that most tranquil week of the whole year, into those days that stretched quietly from Christmas to the Feast of the Holy Name when, as if by common agreement, all of life stopped and rested. The phone rang almost not at all. Even illness, we noticed over the years, took a rest for the holiday. The mail was light on those days when it did come, and always social rather than fiscal—"Dear Uncle Sam and Aunt Phyllis, Thank you for . . ." The tins on the counters were still reassuringly full of sweets, and the refrigerators, no longer stressed to bursting, were nonetheless able to provide easy meals on demand. I read and dozed and indulged in the luxury of daydreams while the quarrel-free children enjoyed new toys and each other. Sam went seldom to the city, his hours in the office and at the hospital both cut to their shortest of the year. . . .

Outdoors the weather was bitter cold that first winter as it continued always to be following Christmas, even in our milder years after that. It was the Feast of St. Stephen. By breakfast the first child had already one-fingered "Good King Wenceslas" out of the old *John Thompson's Primer for Beginners* on the piano in the front hall. As I cooked the eggs and warmed the last of the Christmas coffee cakes, I let myself float in the familiar tune and in the heady security of repetition. For over twenty years some child or other had beat out that tune on the same piano from the same *John Thompson* while I scrambled eggs and stretched leftover pastries by adroitly cutting them into sufficiency. The younger children always did it without suggestion or premeditation. That was the miracle, and life was terribly, terribly good as I stood inattentively stirring the eggs.

We sat to eat, Sam in his overalls and flannel shirt, I in my jeans and big woolly, the children variously attired in footed sleepers, PJs and sweat-suits according to their age and relative condition of alertness. We ate and drank and looked for all the world like a Norman Rockwell come to life. I, who had spent a lifetime deploring that fallacious romanticist, cruised easily into being a jeans- and flannel-clad part of his reality. Life was indeed good, and one should engage in some sentimentality on the Feast of St. Stephen.

The meal over (even adroitness can do only so much), I began to clear the table. The children scattered to dress and to consider how little they could pick up in their rooms without serious consequences. Sam booted up for the barn. He needed to move some more hay down from the loft into the paddocks so the boys could get at it more easily, and the feeding tray for the cottonseed meal needed to be rebraced. I watched him from the kitchen window as he clomped across the yard and down the path between the garden and the orchard, carrying his hands, as he always did, tucked for warmth inside the bib of his overalls. Long before he got to the pasture gate, the cows had heard him and began moving toward him. By the time he opened the gate, they were all there waiting to be patted and scratched and slipped a rotten apple or two from the orchard. Before he relatched the gate, I lost him in a sea of cows. He reappeared at their head and together the whole mass walked toward the barn.

I finished the cleanup and briefly considered being stern about the wrinkled messes that were only half-made beds; but then I gave that up as not worthy of the season and started some wash instead. I was just beginning to meditate on writing some Christmas notes when I realized Sam had been gone for quite a while. Not a lover of the cold, it's unusual for him to work in the open air of December for a couple of hours without coming in to warm up. More to the point, holiday or no holiday, he had to make rounds sometime this morning on the few patients caught in the hospital over the Christmas break. I called John to go check on him and began to assemble my pens and special Christmas notepaper. . . .

In no time at all (even before I found the special gold pen I had bought the week before to use on the green paper) John was back in the kitchen door grinning from ear to ear, his cheeks fiery red and the tops of his ears glowing almost as much as his smile. He beat his hands together, his gloves still on, and hollered at me.

"Daddy says get everybody dressed and come quick!"

I hollered back, "Why?" but he was gone as boisterously as he had come, slamming the door behind him.

"Come on, everybody." I stood at that acoustically magic spot in the kitchen from which my voice can go both upstairs to the bedrooms and downstairs to the family room simultaneously.

"Get your coats on quick. Daddy wants us." Then I remembered to add, "Get your gloves too!"

Every room below and above me gave up its supply of Tickles, and every combination of jeans, PJs, flannels and woolies stopped at the back door to wiggle into boots. We went forth, all of us still struggling with something—a boot, a glove, a pajama leg still caught halfway up a jeans leg—but we went forth.

As we made it into the pasture and halfway to the barn, we saw John's head cresting the hillock that blocked our view of the close below. As John topped the rising, Sam emerged, head first, behind him. And on his shoulders, wrapped around the back of his neck and held there by his gloveless hands, he carried something. The smile on his face was greater even than John's, and he came across the hillock crest with a spring in his gait that I hadn't seen there in years.

The children stopped where they were, and Mary, eighteen and home from college, whispered, "It's a calf!"

That was all it took. The troops broke and ran toward Sam, following him like a swarm of dancing dervishes as he led his triumphant procession into the barn. The stall was instantly a center of warmth and activity as a dozen hands tried to touch and stroke. Behind us I could hear our cow, named Silly Sally, bawling her way up the hillock (it was, after all, *her* calf), making her way toward the barn. The children were enchanted and totally forgetful of us when Sam turned to me, the grin still filling his face.

"We've made it," he said.

"We've made it," I answered and left.

The land had borne well for us that first summer. Our cupboards were full of Mason jars of beans and beets and peaches; the bins with potatoes, onions, even pears and green tomatoes; the freezer with fruit and squash and corn. But this was our first calf. Our herd had reproduced, and the result was life.

I rounded the barn and got to the garden side of it before I began to cry. As soon as I had managed to swipe away some of my tears with my sleeve and quiet some of my heaving by holding onto the barn, I watched as my family came out. Mary first, a tissue held defiantly to her face. Laura next, running for the house. Even John, quiet as he never is, slipping around to the other side of the hay feeder to make a great show of loving Silly Sally by burying his face in her side. The two Sams eventually came out, and Rebecca with them, riding the way the calf had done, astraddle her father's shoulders. And they came singing, Sam's rich baritone breaking over the meadows, "Good King Wenceslas looked out, on the Feast of Stephen . . ."

Before the day was done, Philip would drive out from town for dinner, and we would call Nora in Knoxville with the news. We would also call every schoolmate we could think of, and the whole miracle would be told again and again to people who probably still don't understand why a calf was so important, so singular an occurrence.

When the children had all finally gone off to their beds, I settled into a warm tub, drawing the day and the comfort around me. In a big family a new baby gets to be so ordinary, especially for the older children who have seen it time and again and who know what it means in lost sleep and increased work. They may joke about swelling bellies and pregnant mamas, but they have no anxiety beyond dreading the first year with another infant sibling—and they certainly have no sense of wonder. "The youngest of us is two. So, of course, Mother is pregnant. What else is new?"

Somehow I hadn't realized over the years that the meaning of Christmas had diminished for them as a result, that the joy everyone else spoke of and reported and sent us greeting cards about had become incomprehensible to all of us from sheer habit. Soaking in the tub, I understood that Silly Sally had given back to us the joy of birth.

As I crawled into bed, I poked Sam to wake him. "Merry Christmas," I said as he grinned and took me in.

"HE WANTS YOU
TO HAVE THIS"

EARL WEIRICH

It had been the loneliest Christmas of my life. All my years of partying and hanging out with the wrong crowd had cost me my family and friends. I thought about the revolver lying in my dresser drawer. *Is that my only choice?* I took a deep breath, and decided to take a walk to clear my head.

In the bitter cold I trudged along the streets of Harrisburg, Pennsylvania, where I was the city editor of the local newspaper. It was 1966. I had had so much going for me. After serving in the Marines I went to school and worked my way up the reporting ranks. But what good was success now?

I wandered far from my apartment toward the outskirts of the city, in a deserted area with few streetlights. I thought of families snug in bed after a day of festivities. I had thrown all that away. *God, wherever You are, I'm willing to change everything. Please, give me hope*, I pleaded.

Then I saw a pair of headlights penetrating the darkness. A car stopped across the street from me. The driver got out. I tensed, and knotted my fists inside my trench coat pockets as he approached.

He thrust a small book at me. "God has sent me to give you this."

"Who are you?"

"It doesn't matter," he replied. His voice was gentle. "God loves you. He wants you to have this. Go home and read Romans 8:28."

"Wait a minute," I said. "Do I know you?" It was so dark I couldn't make out his features.

"Romans 8:28," the stranger called over his shoulder as he headed back to his car.

My reporter's instinct kicked in: *I'll follow him. When he opens his car door and the light comes on I'll get a better look at his face.* I reached the curb just as he opened the door. But no light came on. He started the motor and drove away.

A chill that was more than the December cold rushed over me.

Back at my apartment I didn't even take off my coat before plopping down on my bed with the Bible the stranger had given me. I turned to the Book of Romans, then the eighth chapter, twenty-eighth verse: "And we know that all things work together for good to them that love God, to them who are the called according to his purpose."

On the darkest Christmas of my life I found what I had been praying for: A messenger had brought me the gift of hope.

CHRISTMAS
CORRECTIONS

BETTY MALZ

T J. and Maureen O'Bannan were living in quaint Gatlinburg,
Tennessee, during the Great Depression. It was Christmastime, but
the peacefulness of the snowy Christmas card scene outside their
home contrasted with the inner unrest they were both experiencing.

T.J., for his part, was rebelling against oppressive economic priva-
tions by joining his brother in plundering and stealing; while Maureen,
devastated by the change in her husband, pleaded with him to change his
lifestyle. She would rather have him safe at home with her, she told him,
than have all the money in the world. But T.J. insisted he would be a good
provider for her, no matter what it took.

When he and his brother learned that the railroad office would be
holding the payroll and cash receipts over the holiday, they determined to
break in. As they formed their plans, Maureen prayed faithfully for her
husband: "Whatever it takes, Lord, bring him to You."

The nighttime break-in went as planned. But just as his brother was
securing the money in the rumble seat of their Model T Ford, T.J. heard
the sound of a police siren cut through the darkness. He ran for the auto-

mobile, but saw he couldn't make it. He shouted for his brother to drive off, then fell to the ground as a bullet grazed his left cheek.

When he refused to reveal the identity of his accomplice or the whereabouts of the money, T.J. was convicted of the robbery alone and sent to prison. The money, he and his brother agreed, would remain hidden. Maureen visited him as often as she could, and prayed for him constantly.

Three Christmases later, the hard shell around T.J.'s heart began to crack. He awoke at three one morning with an overwhelming desire to make his peace with God. If only he could get to the prison chapel and pray!

"Oh, God," he called aloud through his tears, "have mercy on me." Then he called for a guard, hoping he could convince him to take him to the chapel, despite the lateness of the hour.

A silent, bearded guard appeared, one other than the regular night guard, someone T.J. did not recognize. He seemed old for such a job—indeed, his silvery hair appeared almost radiant—but the twinkle in his silver-blue eyes distinguished him as alert and capable.

Wordlessly the guard opened the cell door and walked beside T.J. to the chapel. Once there, T.J. fell across the altar and asked Jesus to forgive him. The guard, kneeling silently alongside, put his arm around T.J.'s shoulders until T.J. was ready to return to the confinement of his cell. He was peaceful at last in the new freedom of God's forgiveness.

But before the elderly guard could reopen the cell door, they heard shouts. Two uniformed guards ran down the passage, grabbed T.J. and threw him into his cell.

"How did you get out?" they demanded through the bars. "Were you trying to escape?"

"Of course not," responded T.J. "This guard accompanied me to the chapel." But when he looked to his bearded friend for confirmation, the elderly guard had disappeared.

T.J. described him to the others as best he could remember, but neither believed him. One stated flatly that in twenty-six years in that institution he had never worked with an older, bearded guard with silver hair.

Later in the spring, when his case was reviewed before a judge, T.J. agreed to return the money to the railroad. He was released under parole and allowed to go home.

Did an angel help T. J. O'Bannon in his moment of desperation? I have no doubt: Surely a ministering angel was sent to meet the need of this lost soul in response to his wife's intercession, just as the writer to the Hebrews described: "[God] makes his angels winds, his servants flames of fire" (Hebrews 1:7, NIV). Maureen had never given up hope that the Lord would act, and continued to pray for T.J.'s salvation no matter how grim the circumstances.

POSTAGE-STAMP ANGELS

COLLEEN MESSINA

I'm making a card for Grandpa!" my five-year-old son announced.

"That's great, Michael," I said. "We can send it to him in Ohio." My father had left Montana the night before to spend Christmas with my sister's family near Bucyrus, and the children missed him. Mom was already in Ohio, but Dad had stayed behind to finish up some work. My two-year-old, Tiffany, held up the Christmas card she was working on. "It's beautiful," I said. "Show your father." Then the phone rang. "Hello?"

"Colleen?" The strange catch in my mother's voice told me something was wrong.

I felt my stomach tighten as I listened to her tell me about the accident. After driving all night, Dad had fallen asleep at the wheel outside Toledo, swerved into oncoming traffic and collided head-on with a truck. He wasn't wearing a seat belt. "He seemed fine at first when I met him at the emergency room," my mother said, her voice shaking. "Talking and joking, filling out hospital forms—you know your dad. Then four hours later he slipped into a coma. They think he had a head injury and the effects just didn't show up right away." Mom paused, then continued, her voice almost a whisper. "Colleen, he's on a respirator and not responding to anything, not even me."

When I hung up I took my husband Perry aside to explain what was wrong. I wasn't ready to lose my father. I wanted to go hiking through the Montana woods with him again, and listen to him count all the different kinds of angels in the world. "Healing angels, protecting angels, angels for science and music and math. Don't ever be afraid to ask for their help," Dad would say. Now I begged God to send His healing angels to help Dad.

In the days that followed I felt helpless, being far away from my parents who needed me. I wanted to fly to Ohio immediately, but Mom asked me to wait. "He probably won't come around right away," she said, "and I'll need you more later." There was no way of knowing what kind of physical or emotional damage Dad might have when he awoke from the coma—if he awoke. I agreed to stay in Montana a little longer.

The kids knew something was terribly wrong. "Is Grandpa in heaven?" Michael asked, confused when I tried to explain what a coma was. "Is Grandpa crying?" Tiffany wanted to know, looking as if she were about to break into tears herself. We needed to do something for Dad so the kids wouldn't feel so hopeless, so I wouldn't. I'd read that hearing is often the first sense to return to a comatose person.

"Why don't we make a tape for Grandpa?" I asked the kids.

I got out a tape recorder. Holding the microphone tightly, Michael, who had inherited his astrophysicist grandfather's love of science, described his new microscope set. When her turn came, Tiffany told him about the dollhouse her dad had built especially for her. Perry unwrapped a gift so Dad could hear the rustling of the paper. Even our cat recorded some meows.

Now came the hard part. What would I say to him? I opened up my Bible and chose a passage describing Ezekiel's vision of God. Dad loved all the biblical references to fire. "And I saw the color of amber as the appearance of fire

round about. . . . As the appearance of the bow that is in the cloud in the day of rain, so was the appearance of the brightness round about." Then I added, "I don't think it's your time to go, Dad. We need you too much."

I turned off the tape recorder. Taking out the tape, I felt peaceful but drained. I barely had the energy to wrap up the package. Rather than driving to the post office, I put it in the mailbox with a note asking the postman how much postage would cost. When I went out to the mailbox the next day, the package was gone, but there was no bill! Our postman had just taken it. Alarmed, I called the post office. They said it would arrive in Ohio with postage due. *Oh no!* I thought. *What if Dad never gets it?* I remembered his endless list of all different kinds of angels. "God, please have your postage-stamp angels deliver the tape," I asked. Dad would have liked that prayer.

A few days later I got a call from Mom. The package had arrived at their house safely. "How much do I owe you for postage?" I asked.

"I'm looking at the package now," Mom said. "There's no postage on it. Just a postmark!"

My mother set up a tape recorder next to Dad's hospital bed and played the tape continuously. In a few days, the nurses noticed him smiling from time to time. "He's coming out of the coma," they told Mom. During long months of therapy, I finally did go to visit. Dad made a complete recovery. As soon as Mom and Dad got back home to Montana, they came over for a celebration. The kids said it was like having Christmas again.

Dad took me aside. "I know I'm here by grace," he said. "When I was in the coma, I could hear your voice, Colleen. And I saw a magnificent, golden rainbow. That's when I really started to fight for my life. Somehow I knew it wasn't time for me to go yet." Or time for us to let him.

FOUR GUARDIANS

SHEILA J. HUTCHERSON

Joe C. Hutcherson, my father, always had a story, and everybody loved listening to him. But he couldn't tell his stories anymore. He'd been unable to talk for four months because of a stroke. Now he was in the hospital, losing his battle with cancer. He'd left instructions that no life-sustaining measures were to be used, and in the last several days he'd begun refusing medicine and food. We took turns at his bedside—my mother; my brother Michael, who had come from Texas; my sister Linda, from Virginia; and me. I was a nurse and had finished a twelve-hour shift at the hospital just hours before, but I was going back for the night. We all knew Dad had made the decision to die.

The previous week I'd had lunch at a restaurant, and noticed that the adjoining country store was decorated for the holidays. I couldn't help browsing for a while. My eyes were drawn to a large Christmas tree covered with angels. When I saw small brass angels, each playing a musical instrument, I thought immediately of my neighbor Grover Gilbert. Grover prayed aloud whenever he visited my father. "Dear God," he would say, "we thank You for these four angels, one at each corner of the bed, who stand guard over Joe." Goose bumps rose on my arms every time I heard that prayer. Grover seemed so sure the angels were there, and I wanted Dad to see them too. The brass ornaments would be a start, I decided. "I'll take four," I said to the clerk.

"Look, Dad, your angels!" I said that afternoon. I taped them up on the wall in front of my father, their faces shining directly at him. But the tape didn't hold. Every time I looked, the angels were falling. During the week I tried stronger tape, and still they came loose. When I arrived one day I discovered a nurse had hung them from the top of his IV pole. Perfect. But still they wouldn't hang right. The slightest air current in the room twisted the angels this way and that. Invariably their backs were turned toward my father. We straightened them constantly to keep them facing Dad, but they seemed to have minds of their own.

They were still moving every which way that December night when I got to Dad's room. "Mom was exhausted," my brother told me, "and I convinced her to go home." We were all exhausted. In my years as a nurse I'd seen many people die. But this, of course, was different. This was my father.

Dad groaned each time he moved. His once strong hands were now limp and swollen. His face, always so filled with kindness, was now ravaged with pain. Somewhere between two and three o'clock in the morning I looked at Michael standing across the bed from me, and said, "We should pray." My brother and I held hands and shared prayers of thanksgiving for our father's life. My words at the end were the words of our friend Grover. "Thank You," I said, "for the angels who guard him, one at each corner of his bed."

My father's eyes were cloudy. *What does he see?* I wondered. Touching his face, I whispered, "It's okay, Dad. The angels are with you." I pointed at the shiny brass figures hanging from his IV pole. Slowly he turned to look. Suddenly my father's expression became animated. He shifted sideways in bed, his gaze fixed on the angels twisting and turning in the air. Then, eyes half open, still staring at the shiny brass ornaments, he fell asleep. He seemed to be peaceful for the first time in days.

I lay down on the couch in the corner, pulling a sheet around me. Michael sat at Dad's bedside. Dozing in and out of sleep, I felt someone walk past me. Moments later I heard Michael calling, "Sheila, come quick."

I jumped to my feet. Michael was standing with his hand on Dad's chest. "I think he's gone," Michael said. Dad's eyes were slightly open, but he wasn't breathing. I felt for a pulse, but there was none. We called the nurses.

My father was just as I'd seen him before I went to sleep, his body sideways, his gaze fixed on the angels at the top of the IV pole. I closed his eyes. Michael made phone calls to our family, and we sat together to wait.

As I looked at Dad and then at the brass angels, something caught my attention. The four figures were motionless, their faces turned toward my father. The angels who had constantly twisted this way and that were now perfectly still, their gazes fixed.

I felt goose bumps on my arms. "Michael," I asked, "did someone come into the room just before you called me?"

Michael shook his head. "No one."

Except Dad's angels. He'd seen them after all. And I would have loved to hear him tell that story too.

CHAPTER ELEVEN

SPREADING TIDINGS OF JOY

We hear the Christmas angels
The great glad tidings tell . . . .

The Gospel writer needed two adjectives to describe the angel's Christmas message to the shepherds: "I bring you *good* tidings of *great* joy, which shall be to all people" (Luke 2:10). Phillips Brooks used the same pattern. The Christmas angels spread what? *Great* and *glad* tidings.

All the stories in this section have two things in common. The angelic messages are *heard*, and they bespeak *joy*.

Mary Hertzog's first short anecdote is a light-hearted reminder of "where the joy comes from." The chapter ends with delightful stories of music used by God to communicate His heaven-sent *joy*.

— E.B.

"WHERE DO YOU THINK THE JOY COMES FROM?"

MARY HERTZOG

Sitting in the last pew at the back of the church at the midnight service, I half-listened to Father McGraw's Christmas sermon. I thought I'd just sneak out for a little fresh air. As quietly as I could I stepped into the aisle.

"Merry Christmas to you, World!" I shouted once outside.

"Merry Christmas to you too!" I gasped and turned around. *Who said that?* Then I saw him, standing under a streetlamp: a guy in a sheepskin jacket, laughing at me. He looked older than I was—maybe nineteen.

"Why aren't you at church?" he asked.

"I just can't get into it," I said. "That's not what Christmas is about." We sat down on the curb. "Christmas is about . . . joy!"

"Where do you think the joy comes from?" he asked. "From Christ, born on Christmas Day."

I wondered if this guy was for real and looked into his eyes. They were the deepest blue, like the ocean. "Jesus wants you to be happy," the guy went on. "He wants you to be with him like He's always with you." He sounded so sure of himself. But gentle, like he really wanted me to understand what he was saying. Much as I was enjoying his company, I wanted to get back to church. The guy touched my forehead. "Take care, Mary," he said.

I didn't look over my shoulder as I hurried back to the church. I had never told the guy my name.

YABBA-KA-DOODLES!

MIKE MASON

I n a low mood two days before Christmas, I set out to have breakfast with my friend Chris Walton. Chris is that rarest of people, someone who always blesses me. No matter what he's going through, what mood he's in, or what we do together, somehow I always leave his company feeling brushed by heavenly light. As we aren't able to see each other often, our times together are all the more precious.

Despite my gloom that day, in Chris's presence I gradually relaxed as we talked about favorite books and music, about our families, about Jesus. I particularly recall discussing the Jewishness of Jesus, and how during his life the Bible he had was the Old Testament. The more we talked, the more I sensed a quiet joy tugging at my sleeve like a little child. By the time we rose to leave, though I cannot say I felt entirely happy, a change was stealing over me, a warming. Still, it was the sort of thing that might easily have been snatched away by the next small annoyance, were it not for the strange event that transpired in the parking lot of the restaurant.

We were standing beside our cars, Chris by his door and I by mine, saying our good-byes. Traffic rushed past, making it difficult to hear our farewells. But as Chris raised his hand in a wave and beamed a last, broad smile, I distinctly heard him call out, "Yabba-ka-doodles!"

Yabba-what? What did he mean? What language was this? As we'd just been talking of Jewish matters, I wondered if Chris might be delivering some traditional Yiddish greeting.

"What did you say?" I called back.

This time Chris threw back his head, beamed as brightly as if he were seeing an angel, and belted out, "YABBA-KA-DOODLES!"

Chris isn't much given to spontaneous ecstatic utterances. Maybe he was just goofing off? More puzzled than ever, I left my car and walked around to where he stood.

"I don't get it," I said. "Yabba-ka-doodles. What does it mean?"

"Yabba-what?" said Chris.

"Yabba-ka-doodles. You said Yabba-ka-doodles and I want to know what it means."

"Yabba-ka-doodles? I didn't say Yabba-ka-doodles."

"Then what did you say?"

"I said, 'I'm glad we could do this.'"

"I'm glad we could do this?" I echoed blankly.

For a moment we stared at one another, listening to the sound of this inane, colorless sentence against the rapturous syllables of Yabba-ka-doodles. And then we burst into laughter, wild, hilarious, thigh-slapping gales of it, right there in the parking lot. It was so absurd a mistake, so rich and gloriously unlikely. And partly because of that, it filled us with that unlikeliest of qualities in this darkly unsettling world—JOY!

All the way home in the car I kept muttering, caressing, shouting that silly word—"Yabba-ka-doodles . . . yabba-ka-doodles"—giggling and guffawing like a schoolboy. Talk about joy! More than happy, I felt drunk with joy for the rest of that day. And when Chris and I saw each other next, we nearly jumped into each other's arms, yelling, "Yabba-ka-doodles, brother!"

Who would have believed that so much joy could be contained in one crazy, purely imagined word? Later I wondered: Were my ears playing tricks, or is it possible that Chris, without realizing it, really did say Yabba-ka-doodles? Was he unknowingly used as a messenger of God to me, delivering the joyous news of Christmas in an angelic tongue?

ROSA'S SOLO

ROSA G. SANCHEZ

Early on a cold and rainy Christmas morning a few years back, I was busy wrapping presents and making tamales for our traditional family dinner at my mother's. The telephone rang. "Merry Christmas," I said, picking up.

"Good morning, Rosa. It's Angelita." Angelita was the secretary at our church. "Sorry to bring sad news, especially on Christmas Day," she said, "but Mr. Jaramillo passed away. Could you sing at the wake tonight?"

My heart went out to the Jaramillo family. I knew what it was like to lose someone during the holidays. My own brother Alfredo had died at Christmastime eighteen years ago. He was only thirty-nine. The sudden loss left a hole in my life. I hadn't spent a Christmas since without feeling an underlying sadness. "Of course I'll sing, Angelita. And I'll try to find someone to sing with me." I didn't like singing alone. *How in the world can I find someone on Christmas Day?* I wondered.

I opened the church directory to make some calls. I started with my friend Carmen, but her entire family was visiting. I called Rosa, but she was out of town. Angie was already singing with the community choir. Ezequiel was ill, and Alejandra was giving a party. There was no one to help me.

As a last resort, I asked my husband. "Honey, will you sing with me at Mr. Jaramillo's wake tonight?"

"I can't carry a tune," Bernie said. "I'd knock you off-key." He was right and I knew it. And so it was settled. I would be singing all alone, without even an organ to accompany me.

That afternoon Bernie, our two kids and I went to my mother's house for a traditional Mexican Christmas feast. After dinner we opened presents. As evening grew near, my stomach did somersaults. *Dear Lord, I want to praise You properly on this holy day. Let me sing my best to help ease the pain of Mr. Jaramillo's family and friends.* I left my mother's house, and made my way to the funeral home.

The building was full of people who had gathered to pay their last respects. Not everyone could fit into the small chapel, and some people had to stand in the hallway. This large turnout would be a comfort to the Jaramillo family, I hoped. Yet I remembered how seeing the many people who attended my brother's wake had not brought me peace. Not when he had died so young. I hadn't been able to sing songs of praise in his honor. I hoped that I would be able to do it for Mr. Jaramillo.

The crowd fell silent as I stepped up to the podium. "We are gathered here to pray," I said, "for the soul of José Jaramillo, our brother, and for his family and friends, who mourn his loss." After the first prayers I began to sing "Ave Maria." No one joined in. All I could hear was my own too-strident voice. I tried to soften my tone, to sing as perfectly as I possibly could. The Jaramillo family was counting on me. *Lord, inspire me.*

The words coming out of my mouth became quieter, yet they filled the chapel and echoed into the hallway. My voice took on a tender pitch. I was surprised by its lovely sound. In all my life I'd never sung so well!

I took a deep breath before launching into the next verse. Then . . . wait . . . did I hear other voices singing along with mine? "Ave Maria" filled the room. A choir of angels could not have done better. I thought I heard instruments—a harp, a flute, a trumpet—but where were they coming from?

I looked about the chapel. No one was singing. My voice alone created the music. No instruments played. After each group of prayers I sang another hymn—and a glorious chorus joined me. With every song, my confidence grew. I found my voice. I sang with all my heart, for Mr. Jaramillo and for me. And as I sang, the sadness I always felt this time of year started to fade. There was no longer any room in my heart for it. I was filled with joy.

And I was filled with praise for the loving God who held me in His arms, and held my brother just a little closer.

"THE THOUGHT OF NO MUSIC..."

DORIS CRANDALL

It was Christmas Eve, 1933. Mama was preparing to bake her "hard-times fruitcake," so called because the only similarity to fruit it contained was prunes. But it was, to our family, an extra-special cake. My sisters, Lottie, Vivian, Estelle, Dolly, and I sat around our kitchen table, shelling pecans for the cake.

None of us, except Mama, was enthusiastic, and I suspected her gaiety was partly put on. "Mama," I asked, "why can't Grandma and Aunt Ella, and Aunt Fran and Uncle Hugh, and all the cousins come for Christmas like last year? We won't even have any music unless Joe comes and brings his guitar."

We wouldn't mind not having a Christmas tree because we'd never had one, and Mama and Daddy had prepared us for the possibility of no presents, but the thought of no visitors or music really subdued us. Dolly, age five and the youngest, sobbed.

"Why'd we have to move, anyway?" she asked, sniffling. So Mama again explained her version of Dust-Bowl economics.

"When we had to give up our farm, we were lucky to find this place to rent, even if it is too far for the relatives to come. Don't worry, though,"

Mama reassured us. "Why, God might send us company for Christmas right out of the blue, if we believe strong enough." She began to pit the boiled prunes and mash them.

As we worked, a wind came up and whistled through the newspaper we'd stuffed into the cracks in the corners. A cold gust blasted us as Daddy entered through the back door after doing the chores in the barn. "It looks like we're in for a blue norther," he said, rubbing his hands together.

Later Daddy built up a roaring cow-chip and mesquite fire in the pot-bellied stove in the living room, and we were about to get into our flannel nightgowns when someone knocked on the door. A traveler, wrapped in his bedroll, had missed the main road and stopped to ask for shelter from the storm for the night.

"Mind you," he said, when he'd had a cup of hot coffee, "I don't take charity. I work for my keep. I'm headed for California. Heard there's work to be had there."

Then Mama fixed our visitor a cozy pallet behind the stove. We girls went into our bedroom and all crawled into the same bed for warmth. "Reckon he's the one Mama said God might send out of the blue for Jesus' birthday?" I whispered.

"He must be. Who else'd be out in weather like this?" Lottie said, and Vivian and Estelle agreed. We snuggled, pondered and slept.

At breakfast our guest sopped biscuits in gravy. "I never had a family that I remember," he said. "Can't recollect any name 'cept Gibson. You can call me Mr. Gibson if you want." He smiled, revealing gums without teeth. Seemingly, he had no possessions beyond his bedroll and the clothes he wore, but he pulled a large harmonica from his pants pocket and said, "I've always had this. Want me to play something?"

So Mr. Gibson spent Christmas Day with us, and what a delight he was! He helped with the work, told us stories and played all the beloved Christmas songs on his harmonica. He played by ear as we sang church hymns. After much pleading on our part, he agreed to stay one more night.

The next morning, when we awakened, Mr. Gibson was gone. I found his harmonica on the kitchen table. "Oh, Mama," I cried, "Mr. Gibson forgot his harmonica—the only thing he had."

Mama looked thoughtful. "No," she said softly. She picked it up and ran her palm over the curlicues etched in the metal sides. "I think he left it on purpose."

"Oh, I see," I said, "sort of a Christmas present. And we didn't give him anything."

"Yes, we did, honey. We gave him a family for Christmas," she said, and smiled.

We never saw Mr. Gibson again. Daddy had an ear for music and quickly learned to play the harmonica. Through the years, it brought many a joyful memory of that unforgettable Christmas when God sent us Mr. Gibson right out of the blue—a blue norther, that is.

A JOYFUL NOISE

SARAH THOMAS FAZELI

I was not thrilled about playing holiday music at some nursing home. At fifteen years old, there were ten thousand things I would rather be doing on my first day of Christmas break. None of them included dragging my trumpet and music stand to the Wesley Glen Home for the Elderly to entertain. I had committed to do it as part of my required sophomore service project hours, and my mother insisted I go.

Mom dropped me off in the family station wagon, assuring me that she'd run to the drugstore to fill a prescription and return soon, in about thirty minutes. I turned to her with pleading eyes.

"Go," she said. "You'll make people happy."

I rolled my eyes and slid out of the car. As I walked through the thick, revolving doors into the drab building with fluorescent lights and about ten shades of ivory, white and taupe, I started to panic. *Has Mom left yet? Maybe there is still time to back out. I don't want to do this.*

It wasn't really that I wanted to be off sledding with my friends, or at the mall or movies. Nursing homes made me uncomfortable. My only experience with them had been annual visits to see Grandpa

Grzegorczyk at the Midland Home for the Elderly. Visits with him usually included brief reintroductions by my mother.

"Dad, you remember Sarah? Sarah is the middle child. And this one is Bridget, she is nine and getting tall."

My sisters and I would line up to give an unacknowledged kiss on the cheek or to bestow a skittish hug. After the reintroductions and mandatory embrace, my father would whisk us kids off to the House of Flavors to give my mother time alone with her ailing father. That was my full experience with nursing homes and the people who lived in them.

Lost in the momentary flashback, my cheek held briefly against my grandfather's cool, gaunt face, I jumped when a nurse in white scrubs shouted to me.

"Good, you're here!" she called, ducking into a storage bin for something.

"Uh, have you seen a saxophone or a trombone?" I asked timidly. (My fellow band members and I referred to each other by our instruments.) I may not have wanted to be there, but at least I wouldn't be alone. I scanned the foyer for signs of the rest of the brass trio.

But the nurse was doing a million things at once and didn't hear my question. Instead, she rushed past me, arms full of linens. Turning around halfway down the hall, she called out, "Cafeteria's down the hall, to the right!"

I wandered, uncertain, through the corridors. I tried to resist looking in the individual rooms, but most doors were open and I caught glimpses of still bodies and slack-jawed faces. Some of the residents slept, some stared at the television screen and some gazed out toward the hall. I was catching too many glances by looking into the rooms, so I glued my eyes to the floor and continued the search.

I found the cafeteria, led there by the unsavory aroma of reconstituted mashed potatoes, defrosted turkey slices and some kind of Veg-All dish. As I turned into the room, a sagging candy cane garland bopped me in the face. An artificial Christmas tree with paper ornaments stood against the backdrop of institutional furniture. Attendants in white emerged from the kitchen, balancing stacks of trays and distributing them to the people quietly waiting at the tables or in wheelchairs.

Where was the rest of my trio? Did I get the time wrong? Had the concert been canceled? I couldn't very well play a brass version of "God Rest Ye Merry Gentlemen" without the harmony line. I would sound stupid. I'd just have to explain that I couldn't play without the other two musicians.

But before I could excuse myself, a voice rang out, "Ladies and gentleman, we have a special guest today from Bishop Watterson High School. She has come to play the Christmas music for our holiday party!"

I froze. In that moment of confusion, I glanced around and spotted an old upright piano sitting off to the side of the room.

I went to the piano and sat down. The white keys were discolored and some of the black ones were chipped. When I played a few scales, I was surprised to find the instrument was mostly in tune.

But I had no sheet music and hadn't played the piano in ages. I would just have to wing it and rely on musician's memory.

"Joy to the World" came to me first, and then "O Christmas Tree." I played basic versions and had to improvise in places, but it sounded all right.

I had just launched into the second verse of "Silent Night" when I felt a warm presence beside me on the piano bench. A blue-sleeved arm belonging to a very old man rested next to mine. *What does he want? I* wondered. *Does he think I'm someone he knows?* Not knowing

what to do, I continued playing until I saw his large, gnarled hands extend toward the keys.

He turned his head and looked into my eyes.

"Um, hello," I stammered. "Do you, uh, play the piano?"

Slowly, he looked down, staring hard at the keys.

I tried again, "I'm not very good. I just play the trumpet now, in the school band."

His silence made me feel even more awkward. The only way to relieve my discomfort was to start playing again. I raised my hands but hesitated when I saw his hands tremble.

Silence.

Then music. Beautiful music.

Grand, sweeping melodies filled the hall. His hands crossed over each other, stretching to reach the lower notes. *Chopin? Grieg? Liszt?* A familiar classical piece, rich with crescendo and pianissimo, alive with passionate glissandos. He barely looked at his hands as they floated over the ivories, up and down the keyboard. I couldn't take my eyes off them.

The nurses, who a few moments earlier had been rushing around, had stopped all activity. In fact, the whole room was at a standstill. Forks were put down, and even the kitchen workers had stopped to watch and listen.

He went on for almost ten minutes and finally, delicately revealed the ending of the piece. He humbly rested his hands in his lap, looking down. The room was charged, the notes still reverberating in the air.

I whispered, "That was beautiful. They must love having you around here."

A nurse appeared next to us, her face electric. "Oh, John!" She beamed. "We didn't know you could do that!"

I turned to the woman, confused.

"Are you new here?" I asked.

"No, I'm not new." She smiled.

"Oh. Is John new here then?"

The woman leaned closer to me and, our faces nearly touching, said pointedly, "I have been here for fourteen years. John has been here eleven. Never has he so much as touched that piano. We had no idea he could play at all, let alone like that."

Another staff member approached me, her hand on my arm. "What did you do? What did you say to him?"

"Nothing," I said. "I just sat here and played."

"You must have done something!" they both pressed.

"I've got to get Kathy!" one of them said, running toward the reception desk.

Then, John drew my hands together and held them in his. I wasn't afraid; I felt profoundly connected to him. In that moment, I felt the presence of the grandfather I had embraced but never known, and I realized the reason for my being there that day.

Gently, John squeezed my hands and let them go. He set his wrists above the keys and began to play again. I slid off the bench to give him room. I watched for a while as the whole room lit up with the joy of music. Gathering my things, I reluctantly made my way out to my mom, waiting in the parking lot for me.

"How did it go?" Mom asked.

"Fine," I said, too embarrassed and emotional to tell her what had happened.

But I will never forget how a Christmas chore became a Christmas

miracle when two strangers, one in the blush of life and one nearing the end, joined hands and hearts to make a joyful noise that still echoes in my soul.

CHAPTER TWELVE

BRINGING GOD'S
PRESENCE TO US

O come to us, abide with us,
Our Lord Emmanuel!

P hillips Brooks ends his "O Little Town of Bethlehem" carol with the word *Emmanuel*, a name that means "God with us." This puts an odd twist on his concluding prayer, a request followed by a statement: "Abide with us, God with Us!" Is God, through the power of the Holy Spirit, with us today? Yes. Even so, can the Spirit sometimes swoop upon us in a special way? Yes.

These stories illustrate ways in which God's messengers assure us of God's presence. In Linda Maurer's case, the angel literally swooped through the air on an icy afternoon. Charlene Ann Baumbich felt "lifted into the presence of Jesus" when she encountered—what?—a bearded man in a red suit. And for Margaret Newton—well, just who was walking with her family that Christmas Eve, 1955? Janice Brooks-Headrick heard a Christmas carol—but from where? The last story is in some ways the best, because here the silent message comes from the center of a crèche; the Bethlehem babe brings a woman to her knees, adoring the Christ who makes Christmas holy.

−E.B.

SNOW ANGEL

LINDA MAURER

There had been no mention of snow in the Detroit area forecast that drab December day, but I was not surprised when I saw a few stray, bulky flakes drift down outside my Southfield office window about midday. Snow is never far off during our long Michigan winters. By 1:00 P.M., when I walked to my little 1995 Ford Escort in the parking lot, curtains of snow gently fell—beautiful flakes, each one the size of a nickel, fluffy and moist, the kind I used to catch on my tongue when I was a young girl and life seemed simpler. I watched one settle on the back of my glove, its crystalline symmetry quickly dissolving.

Only a bit of green finish showed through the blanket of pristine white that covered my subcompact, and I was a little sad to ruin the igloo effect by opening the door. I started the engine and cranked up the defrost, front and rear. My wipers brushed the windshield clear. As I pulled out onto Franklin Road, headed for a business appointment in the nearby suburb of Royal Oak, the snow blew off my front hood in wisps of white.

I merged cautiously onto the I-696 expressway, feeling my tires slip. *Good thing for this front-wheel drive*, I thought. As I passed a shopping mall my mind drifted to the Christmas rush that was in full swing. Ever since my divorce eleven years ago, I always felt a little lost in the seasonal swirl. The holidays made me feel alone. This year would be the first that my daughter, Becky, twenty-two, who was attending Bible college in Alaska, would not be with me. My son Bill, twenty-four, had become engaged at Thanksgiving to a terrific young woman; that meant he would be spending a lot of time with his future in-laws. Five years before, I had moved in with my ailing parents to help care for them. I barely had any time to do the shopping and holiday cooking for all three of us, and would have no time at all to help out at my church.

My job as a public relations support representative for a computer software company keeps me going, and I love it. But by nature I am a homebody. I couldn't help remembering that when I was a married, stay-at-home mom, I handmade almost all my Christmas gifts. I crafted wood, did ceramics, baked, sewed, arranged flowers. Now I had to fight the throng at the mall, feeling very much alone in a crowd.

I shook off these thoughts and concentrated on my driving. I-696 was heavy with cross-county traffic, especially trucks. On the northwestern rim of Detroit the roadway dips below the urban sprawl through a kind of concrete canyon that goes on for several miles. I always felt claustrophobic on this stretch, rushing between the high walls in packed traffic, with no way to turn off except the narrow ascending exit ramps.

Staying in the right lane, I held my speed below the limit, moving warily through the flying snow. Visibility grew worse by the minute. In the left lane a huge tractor-trailer gained on me. I felt the speeding semi's roar before I heard it. *Why is he driving so fast in these conditions?* I wondered as the cab pulled beside me, flinging a spray of dirty frozen slush across my windshield. As I slowed down to let him by, the truck began to edge into my lane. *Doesn't*

he see me? I squeezed the steering wheel tightly and tapped the brakes. If I hit the pedal hard I would spin out of control on the icy road. I slanted closer to the wall, practically rubbing the concrete. The tiny chirp of my horn was lost in the rumble of the massive truck, whose rear section swayed inches from my window. It was all happening so fast! I was trapped!

"Thy will . . . " was all of a prayer that flew from my lips. I waited for the scream of scraping metal. Then, in front of me, in a swirl of ice and snow, a form took shape before my eyes. Translucent yet unmistakably solid in form, he gathered himself from the blowing crystals of snow and ice. His sweeping robes seemed made from concentrated wind. His magnificent wings glittered and arched heavenward, his very embodiment exuding strength beyond imagining—yet there was no fear within me, only a secure, accepting calm.

Strangely perhaps, I assumed he had been sent to escort me from this life. My fingers loosened their death grip on the wheel and my shoulders sagged. But instead, amazingly, in one fluid movement, he placed his massive right hand on the side of the careening truck and put his left hand on my fender. His left wing enfolded my car and with effortless power he eased the truck back into its lane. Then, as quickly as he had taken shape, he dissolved.

I made it to the next exit ramp, pulled off and sat quietly for a few breath-catching minutes, thanking and praising God. *What a wonderful God You are!* I thought. How could I ever feel alone with such a God protecting me?

Even in the holiday rush, when I sometimes feel abandoned, I need only remember that underneath all the hectic hype, this is the season that celebrates God's presence in our lives on earth, whether it was a baby born in a Bethlehem stable two thousand years ago or a crystalline angel intervening on a snowy expressway to come between death and life.

"I FELT LIFTED INTO THE PRESENCE OF JESUS"

CHARLENE ANN BAUMBICH

For a long time I've wanted to have my picture taken with Santa as a gift to my grown boys, who I knew would appreciate Mom's sense of fun and adventure. (Right, boys? And if you don't, remember Santa is watching, and Santa will be miffed to learn you don't have those photos of Mom and Santa prominently displayed in your homes, thereby causing Santa to perhaps reevaluate next year's stocking loot!) But the last few years, when I've happened upon a Santa in a mall, the lines have always been too long and I've been in too big a hurry to follow through on this whim.

This year was different. I found Santa alone but for an elf (the photographer), one baby on his lap, and two parents hurling themselves around like goons trying to get their precious one to smile. Inclement weather and hazardous road conditions opened this opportunity. And so I seized the moment and told the elf I'd like to have my picture taken, using the holiday special rate of one five-by-seven and two wallet-size photos for under ten dollars. . . . The elf asked my name and told me the obvious: I would be next—as soon as the threesome either got a good picture or expired from their aerobic drama. (My words, not the elf's.)

"Santa, this is Charlene. She'd like to have her picture taken with you."

"Well, hello, Charlene. Come talk to Santa." He was kind; his face registered no shock or scorn.

"Santa, my gift to you will be that I won't sit on your lap. I'll sit on the cushion next to you."

No arguments from Santa.

The two of us cuddled up for the photo and the flash blinked, announcing completion of my mission.

"Charlene, what would you like Santa to bring you for Christmas?" Santa asked.

I hadn't thought this far ahead; the photo was all I'd wanted. (Not thinking ahead is something I'm famous for, but then, Santa probably already knew that.)

Without batting an eye or hesitating for a moment, the following—which was the total truth—erupted from my lips on this particular Friday.

"Santa, I'm having a hysterectomy next Wednesday, and I'd like swift healing." Although I couldn't believe what I'd uttered, I was not surprised, as this disbelief of my own utterings is routine.

Then Santa's blue eyes looked into mine, as though they were piercing my very soul. He said, "I'll pray for you, and so will Mrs. Claus."

I was so moved that I immediately began to cry. "Oh, Santa, you couldn't have told me anything more perfect." Realizing that I was now standing before him bawling, I added, "Perhaps more estrogen would be nice too."

Santa smiled. I thanked him one last time and walked away, but not before saying, "You know, you still come to my house in the middle of the night every year, even though my baby is twenty-five years old."

"I know," he said.

Well, the photos were swell. But they were secondary to my experience. I told nearly everyone I saw about my meeting with Santa. "It was as though Christ became incarnate in this Santa to assure me that everything would be okay," I heard myself repeating time after time. "I felt so calm." My friend Janet, a sister in Christ whom I'd told, faxed me before my surgery to let me know she was praying for me. She prayed that my surgery go as scheduled. She prayed for my recovery, for my relationships to be a blessing to me and God, for the doctors to have wisdom. And "I pray," she wrote, "that Mr. and Mrs. Claus have their prayers answered." She, too, had been affected by my story.

As it turned out, surgery went pretty well. Two hours after surgery, however, my heart rate began to drop—all the way to zero, which, as one doctor said, "we thought was a little too low." I became a flat-liner on the monitors (which means you're on your way to dead), and nurse Jaci had to administer CPR. I snapped right back, thanks to the grace of God and Jaci's quick actions. I have recuperated just fine.

But I cannot begin to tell you how many times during and since my recovery I've revisited my encounter with Santa. I am in awe of how I felt so blessed and lifted right into the presence of Jesus when Santa talked to me. In fact, God's arms, looking very much like Santa's, can be seen wrapped around me in the photo. Of this I am sure.

"I COULDN'T BEGIN
TO DESCRIBE IT"

MARGARET NEWTON

The traps are set," my husband Claude announced.

Seven-year-old Don tugged his winter boots off and headed to the window, watching for the snow he hoped would fall this Christmas Eve. "Maybe we'll catch some beavers," he said.

Claude nodded and took off his coat. He had never set traps before—in fact, he had never gone hunting or fishing. Usually Claude and Don spent time together reading or bowling, but Claude had started to think he should do something more "macho" with our growing son. Most of Don's friends hunted with their fathers and sold the pelts at the local trading post. In 1955 that was a popular way to pick up extra money in rural Oregon. Claude didn't want Don to feel that he was missing out, so he borrowed some traps from a neighbor and took Don across the pasture to the irrigation ditch to set them. Now it looked like Claude was having second thoughts.

Just past sunset Don let out an excited shout. "It's snowing!" he cried. "The biggest flakes you've ever seen!" I grabbed my camera, and the three of us went outside. After we came back in, Claude stood staring out the window.

I went to start dinner, and Don followed me into the kitchen to set the table. Moments later Claude appeared in the doorway. "Let's go down and spring those traps," he said. I was glad. Dinner could wait.

"Okay," Don agreed cheerfully, pulling his boots on. I got my coat. We sang carols to pass the time while walking back across the pasture. Don admitted he didn't care if he ever caught a beaver—or any other animal, for that matter. Claude said that was just fine. I prayed it wasn't too late. Finally the three of us stood hand in hand beside the ditch.

"All empty," Claude said, relief in his voice. He sprang each trap with a stick and swung the bunch of them over his shoulder for the long walk home. The moon lit a path at our feet, and the three of us followed it through the woods in silence. Don skipped along just ahead. The trees, the moon, the snow—it was perfect, but it was more than that. There was something different about the woods that night. Something all around us, familiar and strange at the same time. It was almost as if someone else were taking our path, walking beside us. I couldn't begin to describe it, not even to Claude.

When we got home Don sprawled out under the Christmas tree to watch the blinking lights. "How about a cup of tea?" I asked my husband, still trying to find a way to describe the presence in the woods. Claude's eyes softened, and a little smile played at the corner of his mouth. "What is it?" I asked.

"I think Jesus walked with us tonight," he said.

"Oh! Is that who it was, Daddy?" Don piped up. "I thought it was an angel."

My husband and son had found just the words I was looking for.

SERENADE AT SUNRISE

JANICE BROOKS-HEADRICK

I had never been more homesick or stressed than that Christmas in 1981, the year my husband Charles and I pulled up stakes and moved to the Texas badlands to work in the vast oil fields of the panhandle. We were thousands of miles away from home for the first time. Our relationship was young, so we didn't have the comfort of long years of habit to smooth over the lumps in life. Money was tight. If I hadn't been madly in love with the man with the turquoise-blue eyes, I would have run home to Mama. As it was, I cried every time I heard "White Christmas."

Texas just didn't look right—nineteen shades of brown, flat, and nary a tree in sight. Charles and I were both mountain-born and raised back east, in Tennessee and upstate New York, respectively. Out in the badlands— with no green hills to hold me in their hollows—I felt as if I might fall off the earth.

Charles had three children from a previous marriage who came along to live with us—Charlie, fifteen, Sherri, fourteen, and Kresti, nine. All were sick for a full three months after the move—measles, chicken pox, tonsillitis. They grew out of clothes faster than they grew into them. Then there was Charles's brother Jim. A gifted musician, Jim had rolled through from the West Coast on his way to Nashville. He stopped in the café where I waited tables and said he would be in town for a few days, sleeping in his car. I offered him our couch. Four months later, Jim was still on the couch.

With six mouths to feed, house and car payments, doctor bills and what have you, we worked countless hours just to make ends meet. One night I woke up crying. I didn't know how to work any harder, any smarter, or make any more money to afford a good old Christmas like back home. This year we just wouldn't have Christmas. It broke my heart.

Not long after, Jim came in from his job at a shop where he repaired drilling equipment to say there was a fellow who needed his wells watched during Christmas. Wells have to be watched when workers aren't around, and they would all be off for the holiday. If the generators go on the blink, the wells can explode. Besides, this fellow had had some tools and expensive equipment turn up missing and he suspected thieves had been sneaking around.

Charles, Jim and I had a quick conference around the kitchen table. "If we take the work," Charles said, "we can afford to celebrate a few days early. Then we'll watch the wells in shifts on Christmas Eve and Christmas, with one of us always here to keep an eye on the kids."

That's how I came to be guarding an oil well my first Christmas Eve in Texas.

Charles's job was to baby-sit the gas well. It needed a practiced eye because gas wells can blow sky-high if anything goes wrong. Jim and I split shifts at the big oil well. He drove me out for my shift with the kids and my feisty keeshond Foxy crammed in the backseat. I had been told there was a trailer with phone, electricity, radio, TV and flush toilets. Still I was nervous. That's why I was bringing Foxy along, as well as the .22 in my purse. I

was worried about those thieves. We were jouncing along when Charlie hollered, "Look!"

In the black-velvet sky shone a single dazzling star. Yes, like everything else in Texas, stars are *big*. But I had never seen anything like the brilliance of that star in the eastern sky. It was the size of my fist. "You think that's the same star the wise men saw?" Charlie wondered aloud. For an instant it really felt like Christmas.

My joy faded, though, when we bounced into the oil well site. It's hard to convey the size, smell and roar of a Texas oil rig. The drilling floor was almost five stories off the ground! Jim went over the checklist with me for the monstrous generators. Set inside a building, they reeked of fuel and made a noise like their name: Waukeshaws. *Wa-kee-sha . . . wa-kee-sha* . . . even with our bulky ear protectors the noise still drummed into my bones.

A vast waste pit contained drainage from the rig. The stench of oil permeated everything. It was about as far from the Norman Rockwell Christmas of my dreams as I could have imagined.

Jim dropped Foxy and me off at the trailer. "See you tomorrow," he said as he and the kids drove off. "Merry Christmas!"

I tried to settle in. I had brought some sewing to do and some snacks. I turned on the TV but reception was bad this far from a transmitter. I thought of my relatives back in Tennessee—cousins, brothers, sisters, nephews, uncles, aunts—all having a joyous Christmas Eve together. I grabbed the phone, thinking to call my folks in New York. *At least we can cry together*, I told myself. The phone was dead.

I hoped robbers wouldn't be out on Christmas Eve. I had Foxy, who would bristle, snarl and snap if there was trouble, though I didn't think she had it in her to attack. Well, I could shoot the thieves—if I had it in me. I checked the pistol. No bullets. Great. I was thirty miles from help, with no car, a phone that didn't work, a dog that wouldn't bite, and a gun that couldn't shoot. *Lord,* I prayed, *please don't forget about me all alone out here.*

It was a good thing I had brought the sewing. The generators wouldn't need checking until morning. I sewed until my eyelids got heavy, then bundled up and went to sleep.

I awoke to dawn drifting in the windows. Sunrise in the desert is wondrous, the colors amplified by the stark landscape. Texans say when God was making the world He ran out of mountains, trees and rivers by the time he got to the Texas badlands. So he just emptied his paint box and gave them the most glorious sunsets and sunrises on earth. I think it takes that kind of desolation to make room for so much beauty.

As a bonus, my favorite Christmas hymn, "Joy to the World," was playing on the radio. Smiling sleepily, I reached to turn it up and was quite surprised I couldn't. The radio wasn't playing. It wasn't even plugged in.

"He rules the world . . ."

It sounded like a huge choir, the soaring voices blending perfectly. I looked at the TV. It too was off. I got up and unplugged it anyway. Still the choir rang out, even over the thrum of the Waukeshaws. It seemed like the sound was coming from everywhere at once.

"And makes the nations prove . . ."

I searched the trailer. There was no radio, no TV, no tape player to account for the ringing chorus of joyous voices. I knew the song by heart and could understand every word the choir sang. Sound carries far in the desert, but thirty miles? Impossible. *It must be coming from outside.*

I wrapped my coat around me and stepped out into the sharp morning

air. Foxy was dancing circles around my ankles, her ears at the alert. We looked and looked for a source. The music seemed to be coming from the east . . . from all of the east.

"No more let sins and sorrows grow . . ."

Was there someone on the other side of the pit? Jim blasting the car radio to wake me up? Foxy and I climbed an embankment. We were completely alone with the most awesome sunrise I had ever seen, even for Texas. The midnight-blue of the sky lightened into vivid colors that spilled across the desert—lilac, cerulean, magenta, sienna.

I sat on the cold, sandy bank, my arm around Foxy, awash with music and light. There were no other intrusions on my senses—no sounds, no smells. Maybe I was hallucinating. Maybe I was reacting to stress and loneliness. When the verses were over, no doubt, the music would fade. But then something happened, something I still can't explain.

The voices swelled into a fourth verse of "Joy to the World." I knew only three verses. Still, I was hearing a fourth as clear as the day that was dawning, with the full force of the invisible cosmic serenade. I cannot remember the words to that verse. They were rich with praise and glory, I know, and clear to me at the time. But today I cannot repeat a single line. (I've checked hymnbooks and discovered a fourth verse—though not the one I heard that morning!) Like the colors of that dawn sky, the words were both tangible and intangible, meant only for the moment yet leaving an impression for a lifetime.

A heavenly host sang that morning out in a Texas oil field. I thought I was alone and forgotten, forced to endure the most desolate Christmas of my life. But God shook me awake with an unforgettable reminder that His glory and the glory of His son are everpresent.

CALL TO WORSHIP

JANET THOMAS BRASWELL

Was it real or was it a dream? I still can't say for certain. All I know is that it happened on the very Christmas when my heart was feeling its smallest, hardest and most envious.

The days before Christmas passed in a queer green haze of self-pity, and the joy I usually felt during the holidays unraveled like an old tattered ribbon.

All I longed for were the things I could not have—the stunning piece of jewelry that my hardworking husband wouldn't be able to give me, the delightful gifts I'd love to shower on family and friends—just this once! The store windows and catalogs mocked me with their glittering displays. I was embarrassed about the inexpensive gifts I presented to the children's teachers, about having to look for cheap wrapping paper and discount cards.

Our daughters, eight-year-old Laura and three-year-old Perrie, were perfectly happy as they cut out construction-paper chains. But I was consumed with a desire for a Victorian tree festooned with tasteful antique ornaments. As I watched the girls arranging our manger scene on the end table in the living room, my thoughts were fixed on fine concerts and galas that we couldn't afford to attend.

On Christmas Eve, even the program at our church left me feeling empty. If only I'd been able to worship in a grand cathedral, I thought as we drove home. If I'd been listening to a magnificent choir while organ chords soared upward—then my spirit would have been lifted and I could have wholeheartedly experienced the presence of Christ's birth.

"Mommy?" Laura was tugging at my sleeve. "I was thinking about baby Jesus," she said. "Let's take him out of our manger scene tonight and put him away somewhere, like he was when he was in heaven. Then in the morning, before we open presents, we can put him in the manger."

"Honey, that's a nice idea." When we got home, Laura took the baby Jesus from the nativity set on the end table. I watched as Laura surveyed the living room and decided that the little wooden Jesus should go up on the mantel for the night—because, as she explained to Perrie, "this is high, like heaven."

After Laura and Perrie fell asleep, Wayne and I rustled around as quietly as possible, setting out their simple packages. I tried to return Wayne's satisfied smile as we went up the stairs to bed, kicked off our slippers and threw back the covers; I didn't want him to know that Christmas this year was falling so short of my expectations.

Much later that night, after several hours of restless tossing and turning in the darkness of our bedroom, I opened my eyes. There was a faint glow in the hall. Puzzled, I eased myself out of bed and padded to the top of the stairs.

Down below the glow was even brighter. Had Wayne left on the tree lights? I crept down the steps. I felt like a child caught up in some strange spell, moving slowly as though underwater. At the foot of the stairs I stopped in wonder.

A warm light radiated from the end table in the living room. Surprised and yet unable to draw back, I tiptoed closer and saw that the source of the light itself was the tiny figure at the center of the manger. "Baby Jesus," I whispered, and fell to my knees on the carpet. As the moments passed, I was filled with a sense of understanding and awe so complete that it erased all feelings that had come before. Gone was my nagging envy. My jealousies were dissipated; the sad corners of my heart were flooded with a profound and satisfying peace. This, I thought, this is what it means to be wealthy.

How long I stayed there I don't know. But finally the light faded and I got to my feet. I found my way back to bed and fell asleep at once.

In the morning, when the children awakened and we trooped downstairs, I gave a startled shiver as I looked in the room. "Baby Jesus!" Perrie cried, rushing toward the mantel. He lay just where Laura had left him the night before. When she lifted the baby down and placed him in the manger, all four of us knelt and bowed our heads.

Was what I'd experienced during the night only a dream? It really didn't matter. Because the ongoing richness of God's presence, in whatever way we are finally led to see it—that is the reality.

(Continued from page iv)